MODERN MOTHERHOOD

Pregnancy, Childbirth & the Newborn Baby

MODERN MOTHERHOOD

PREGNANCY, CHILDBIRTH
& THE NEWBORN BABY

by H. M. I. Liley, M.D.
with Beth Day

Foreword by Virginia Apgar, M.D., M.P.H.

 *Random House New York*

"We are all different—due in part to heredity but also because we were brought up differently. The way we were cared for and treated in early infancy largely shaped our personality, and so, made each of us a different individual."

—from the film *Baby Meets His Parents*
Encyclopaedia Britannica Films

Foreword

The unborn baby has a champion in Dr. H. M. I. Liley. With warmth and wit, common sense and scientific accuracy, she describes the world of the womb all have known but none can recall. She effectively dispels the myths and explains the mysteries of life before birth without ever minimizing the miracle of human development.

To Dr. Liley, the unborn child is never the abstract fetus of the textbooks, nor is the newborn baby the traditional "clean slate," ready to chalk up life's impressions only after delivery. Rather, he is a unique individual with distinctive characteristics and responses to external stimuli long before birth. She sees him as an active partner in pregnancy, labor and delivery. Her description of the birth process from the infant's point of view is the most graphic I have ever read.

Dr. Liley brings impressive credentials to her task. Her professional perception stems from her years of experience as a practicing pediatrician and as director of the Antenatal Clinic, National Women's Hospital, Auckland, New Zealand.

Her understanding of life before birth is enhanced by a working alliance with her husband, Dr. A. William Liley, world-renowned obstetrician who developed the daring procedure of intra-uterine transfusions for infants threatened by Rh complications. Another significant qualification is the fact that Dr. Liley is the mother of five children.

From these combined vantage points, she views the infant world imaginatively, yet realistically, providing fresh insights for the medical profession as well as for potential parents.

VIRGINIA APGAR, *M.D., M.P.H.*
The National Foundation—
March of Dimes

Introduction

All of the best stories are told and retold. The exciting thing about telling this tale today is that we know more about the human baby—unborn and newborn—than we ever have before. Within the past two years the baby finally has come into his own in the medical world, and a branch of medicine, called fetology, is devoted exclusively to the study of the baby from conception on. It is ironic that science has touched the moon before it has answered the basic mystery of human existence: Why is a baby born when he is? What starts labor?

Medicine, in fact, has always managed to put the cart before the horse, concerning itself in the individual disease with dreadful results before attacking the question of prevention; and, in individual lives, investigating senile states and only later working down to the newborn. The great physicians of the past whose teaching has influenced all phases of the profession, treated the noble, the wealthy, and the famous for established disease. Surgery was born to fulfill the demand of warring princes who wanted to keep their mercenary soldiers active in the battlefield. Ordinary men, and, lastly, women and children only became objects of scientifically attested medical attention after the industrial revolution had made individual life economically important. The branches of medicine devoted to the care of women and children—obstetrics, pediatrics, and gynecology—are actually little more than sixty years old. They are so "new" that even as recently as a dozen years ago medical school teachers expected the "bright" students to wish only to become physicians and surgeons.

Before obstetrics took over the handling of maternity cases, the problems of pregnancy and the care of infants were traditionally a mother-to-mother affair; knowledge, techniques, and not a little body of myth were passed from one generation to the next. A woman was supposed to learn the facts of childbearing and child care while still a girl in her mother's home, by watching and helping care for the younger members of the family. As conception control came into general practice, however, and families subsequently shrank in size, fewer girls had any experience with infants in their homes. Trained nurse-maids also became less available to the average young mother, so that the only source of help or advice was the doctor.

A generation ago, in our own mother's day, it was customary for a pregnant woman to commit first herself and then her baby to a doctor who assumed the total management, indoctrinating her with a set of rules. The doctor told her what to do, without bothering to explain why.

The basic error of this approach was soon apparent when mothers discovered, to their dismay, that sets of rules did not work for all babies. No matter how zealously a young mother obeyed her doctor's instructions, success was not necessarily assured. She could do everything she was told to do and still have a hungry, miserable, colicky baby.

As women became increasingly less satisfied with the rule-book technique of handling their babies, they began to ask for more participation in their own pregnancies. New approaches became fashionable, among them the "natural childbirth" school, which claimed to be able to instruct women so that they would have a painless birth. Hospitals established pre-natal classes for prospective parents.

Much of the instruction offered, however, was designed to instruct the mother about the conduct of her labor. Mothercraft teaching, where added to this, tended to be based on the experiences of a nurse who could efficiently bathe and feed twenty nursery babies in a given time, rather than on those of a mother who cared for a family around the clock.

The tremendous emphasis on training for labor and birth is quite unrealistic. As any mother knows, a year or more elapses from the conception of one child until her body is ready to conceive another. Her pregnancy has a phase of receiving or conceiving her child; then a long phase of incubating it; and a relatively short labor and birth phase. Finally it takes another two to three months to return to the non-pregnant state. Surely to dwell too much on the one day of the entire year when she may experience labor pains distorts things quite out of perspective. Intensive training for labor is meant for the connoisseur of labor, not for the average motherly woman who wants a family to have and to hold. Besides, nature or the "natural" way does not necessarily mean that all will go well for the child. Nature is notoriously wasteful, and though the mother may achieve a thrill to the point of ecstasy in delivering her child, her baby may actually suffer considerably more trauma during "natural" birth than he would experience with a carefully "managed" confinement. Labor and birth should be analyzed and explained to the mother-to-be as a part of good obstetric care, but as only one part of a comprehensive course that embraces pregnancy as a whole.

Medically the purpose of obstetrics is to obtain a safe delivery for the mother, and a live child, to counteract the staggering infant-mother mortality rates of the past. In our grandmothers' day, for example, a woman had to resign herself to the fact that out of the ten or twelve pregnancies she would experience during her fertile years, she could hope to raise no more than five children. Today, thanks to adequate medical care for women and babies, better than ninety-six percent of babies (in the Western world) are born alive and healthy. The problem that faces us today, therefore, is not so much the one of securing a living child as it is of understanding the infant.

And how does a young mother without previous experience or trained help cope with her baby?

In our hospital in Auckland, New Zealand, we felt one of the answers to this pressing problem might lie in putting the infants with heir mothers as soon after the birth as the mother's condition would permit, so that the mother would know her baby, and know how to care for him when she took him home. Seven years ago we instituted this new procedure and the baby was brought to the mother within a day or so following the birth. We found, however, that most young mothers were not equipped to receive their infants. The majority had never before held a baby. Only about one in ten had seen a child being breast-fed. Many mothers were frankly fearful of the tiny strangers they had produced.

Once again, we had reversed things. Putting mothers and babies together, we realized, could only be successful if the mothers already knew something about their babies: Why the newborn looks and acts as it does; how it communicates; what it needs. . . .

It was at this time that we created an ante-natal program designed to teach mothers about their babies—both unborn and newborn. While we do include pre-natal physiotherapy training to keep the mother supple and aid her in her labor, the real goal of our classes is to teach the mother about her baby. We tell her what the pregnancy is like from his point of view, what it is like for him to go through the birth, and what he will most need from her when he is born.

Among the many fascinating discoveries that we see among our babies, I think the most important is that each baby is an individual. It is separate and distinct from every other individual, in fact, much earlier than anyone suspected. In treating the unborn we have found that the human fetus possesses distinct characteristics from about the fourth month of intra-uterine life, before his mother even feels him.

In today's small-family, servantless society, few young women have a chance to learn about babies in their homes. Fewer still can look forward to trained help to care for their infants when they bring them home from the hospital. More than women of any other era, today's mothers need to understand their babies so that they will be able to handle them alone with confidence. We can no longer afford them the luxury of a first baby to "learn" on.

It is to mothers-to-be, prospective fathers, and college students of human biology that this book is dedicated. As a mother of five children, as well as a practicing pediatrician, I can personally guarantee that the more prospective parents know about their baby, the happier both they and their baby will be.

MARGARET LILEY

Auckland, New Zealand
March, 1966

Contents

MODERN MOTHERHOOD

Pregnancy, Childbirth & the Newborn Baby

chapter one

FROM THE FIRST CELL
OF LIFE *Two Hundred Million Miracles*

Pregnancy is not merely an experience every woman should have, like graduation from college or travel to Europe. There are many women who live full and successful lives without having any children. There are also women who bear children they resent and despise. The one valid reason to have a baby is because a woman and her husband want a baby. But before this very serious decision is made, there are several things it might be wise to consider.

A baby will not be a little doll to dress up prettily and prop in a carriage and show off to the world. Babies are people. Tiny, to be sure, but quite as distinct in their personalities and demands as adults; a woman can no more make playthings of them, than she could make a toy of her husband. She must be prepared to cope with another individual, human being.

Nor will her pregnancy be entirely her affair. The baby will not prove to be a quiescent little vegetable, slumbering silently in his warm dark world till birth. He is very busy, and rare is the pregnancy in which he does not make the mother well aware of his movements and reactions.

From the moment the baby is conceived, it bears the indelible stamp of a separate, distinct personality, an individual different from all other individuals. Once the baby has started, in fact, there is very little one can do about the kind of person he will be. For we do not breed the children we want. We must accept what we have.

It was once thought that the baby was primarily the creation of the father, who implanted it in the mother, where it was nourished until ready for birth. Another, more feminist view had it that the baby was almost entirely the product of the mother, whose fertility was merely triggered by the male, who, in himself, contributed very little. Grandparents have indulged for centuries in the pastime of studying all the newborn members of the family and happily claiming all the nicest features and characteristics for their side.

In actual fact, except for sex, which is determined by the male sperm, all the inherited components of that first cell of life derive equally from both parents. It is ironic, in light of our modern knowledge of heredity, to think of all the women who were blamed and "put aside" because they failed to produce a male heir. The determination of sex is the only exclusive inheritance from one parent, and it is from the father.

The baby inherits exactly equally from his mother and his father, just as they were the products of their two parents. Pregnancy is, therefore, a shared responsibility, and one of the most interdependent conditions of life. The woman can no more get through her pregnancy successfully without the man than the baby can get along without her.

When the tiny microscopic sperm from the father unites with the mother's ovum and produces a new cell, the entire pattern of a future individual is contained in that minute pinpoint of living tissue. Within the single cell, just able to be seen with the naked eye, there is miraculously contained a blueprint of the physique, coloring, sex, temperament, and much of the future internal pattern of the mature person. Yet there is no man living who can read this blueprint. And it takes from eighteen to twenty-five years for the entire pattern to unfold.

Besides the design for the future the tiny cell contains the potentiality of all that the baby will need for his life within his mother: his placenta, umbilical cord, and amniotic sac (bag of waters), which are all his own, not his mother's. He is the parasite, setting up his living room inside her. She is the host, who provides him space, and eventually nourishment, once he has implanted his placenta into the soft interior walls of the uterus, where it will serve as a way station between his body and his mother's, transporting both food and waste.

From the first single cell, this speck of new life grows rapidly. By the time it reaches the uterus and implants in the spongy lining, the single cell has divided, multiplied, and grown into the ball of cells that is already differentiating into layers, just as the artist's first quick circles delineate what will be a human body. The implantation, which is a process not unlike dropping a seed into well-prepared soil, occurs about the 12th day, just before the mother's next menstrual period is due. In fact hormones produced by the implanting child prevent this menstrual flow.

The first phase of intra-uterine life, during which the cells implant and gradually evolve into a tiny creature— no larger than the father's thumb but nonetheless an individual person—takes place roughly within the first three months of the mother's pregnancy. It is during these first three months, when the tiny organs are forming, that the baby is the most vulnerable.

Because so many very highly complicated processes are taking place, this is the period of pregnancy when something is most likely to go wrong. Drugs taken by the mother or illnesses may affect her baby's development. Or the pattern within the cell may simply fail to emerge in some fundamental way. If the cell fails to develop properly, or to implant properly in the lining of the uterus, the mother's body simply discards it. This is the natural, spontaneous abortion that we commonly call miscarriage.

Hospitals by no means see all of the spontaneous abortions, but on the basis of what we do see, we estimate that roughly twenty percent—or about one in five—of all pregnancies miscarry during the first three months. Since this is such a very common occurrence, a miscarriage, while disappointing, should by no means be discouraging, nor make a young woman fearful about subsequent pregnancies. Unfortunately, there is sometimes an old lady over the fence, or a meddling mother-in-law, who will tell the young newly married woman who has just suffered a miscarriage that it was all her fault. This sort of person will infer that she was not able to carry her baby to term because she's a giddy girl, and has been staying out too late and smoking too much or drinking too much. It's nothing of the sort. Miscarriages during the first three months of pregnancy merely relate to natural percentages. If one fertilized ovum in five is going to abort, then the chances of its being the first one are quite high.

Women who have had one miscarriage often worry unduly that their next pregnancy will also miscarry. It is well to remember that just as each woman is different, and each pregnancy is different, each of one woman's pregnancies is different. For it is the fetus, not the mother, who normally determines the condition of the pregnancy. A woman for example, can carry her first baby successfully to term, then have a second baby that goes into premature labor, and then have a third pregnancy that reaches term. The particular fetus in her second pregnancy dictated the situation, rather than the physiology of the mother herself. One fifth of women who have miscarried once will do so by chance in the successive pregnancy, which means that four percent of all women will miscarry twice in succession. One percent will miscarry three times in a row. And all of these women still have an eighty percent chance of carrying their next baby through to term.

If a woman does have two miscarriages in a row, it is wise for her to have a thorough examination to determine if anything can be found that might have contributed to this. But rarely is anything found to be wrong with the mother. The majority of spontaneous abortions indicate no abnormalities in the mother. They are, like the small percentage of seedlings in a window box that fail to sprout and grow, simply a result of some defect in the initial implantation.

It is also during this early developmental stage of pregnancy, before the cells have taken the shape of a tiny human being, that clinical abortions, if necessary, should be performed. The operation is relatively simple at this time; whereas after the third month of pregnancy, when the baby is firmly entrenched within the womb, abortion becomes much more difficult to perform and is more hazardous for the mother.

Some of the reasons that were once considered medically valid for performing clinical abortion have now, happily, been eliminated by advances in diagnosis and treatment of the unborn. Syphilis, for instance, which was once a serious threat to the healthy growth of a fetus, can now be successfully treated so that the baby is unimpaired. Until diagnostic techniques have been further perfected, the problem of whether to abort all pregnant women who have German measles or who have taken the crippling thalidomide drugs, still remains an ethical one, since fifty percent of the babies thus exposed could develop normally without defects. With the present procedures it would be possible to reduce the incidence of diseases such as hemophilia or some forms of muscular dystrophy by aborting only boy babies, since girls carry the diseases but never suffer from them. However, some unaffected boy babies would also lose their lives if this were done.

It is already possible to determine the sex of the unborn child, through both an assay of the fluid surrounding the fetus and through x-ray. My husband, who specializes in hemolytic diseases of the unborn, frequently discovers the sex of his tiny patients as a by-product of his examinations. He does not, however, divulge this information to the prospective parents. "It would be," he insists, "like opening all your Christmas boxes a month before Christmas!"

Before airplanes were pressurized, it was thought that flying was dangerous for pregnant women. This is no longer true with today's modern aircraft, and in New Zealand air ambulances transport as many pregnant women to hospitals as other types of patients. In 1965 one baby decidedly disproved the theory that altitudes are bad for babies by managing to get himself born on a

Lufthansa flight between Frankfurt, Germany, and New York City. He was charged no fare.

Unborn babies are wonderfully well insulated. Their controlled and bacteria-free environment permits them to withstand ailments and injuries that would lay low an adult—or a baby a few months old. There have been cases where pregnant women have suffered injuries, and been in auto accidents or sustained bad falls, that resulted in fractures of the limbs of their unborn babies. Yet the babies healed quite nicely on their own, within the womb, with no help from a doctor. There are also cases on record where unborn babies were hit with gunshot—and healed within the uterus with no worse aftereffect than a scar.

Fashions in pregnancy have changed with the times, suiting the sentiments, fancies, or fears of the particular age. It was not many generations ago that high-minded pregnant women played soft music, walked on tiptoe, thought noble thoughts, averted their gaze from ugly sights, and strove mightily to contain their tempers for the entire duration of their pregnancy—on the premise that every action, emotion, thought, or experience they had might leave its imprint on their unborn baby.

From that trying exercise in self control, we have swung around in the past decade to the "mothers can hardly hurt their babies" school of thought, perpetuated by doctors in order to relieve their patients of guilt feelings and make them happier throughout their pregnancies by simply "leaving the worries to us."

The truth lies somewhere in between. Since the unborn baby is by no means a somnolent, inert passenger, he is aware of his mother, how she moves, what she does, how she sounds. She can affect him in a number of different ways. The very first good service that she can perform for her new baby, however, is to see to it that she feels as well as possible while she is carrying him.

chapter two

THE FIRST YEAR BEGINS

The Mother's Body Adjusts to Her Invader

Beginning with conception, dramatic changes occur in the mother's body. The internal clocks that tick out the rate of heartbeat, of breathing, even of digestion and elimination, all become geared anew. The menstrual rhythm ceases, gradually in some women, immediately in others. The volume of circulating blood and other body fluids increases.

During the first three months of pregnancy, while the baby is changing from the first cell of life into a tiny human creature, the uterus gradually enlarges from about the size of two thumbs held together to the size of two fists. There is little weight gain during this stage.

It is in the second phase of pregnancy, from the third to the seventh month, that the mother begins to gain. She really gains very rapidly now, at the average rate of about one pound per week, which gives her a total increase of sixteen pounds at the end of the seventh month.

This weight is not all fetus. Even at term, the baby, his placenta, and the bag of waters do not weigh over twelve pounds, which should represent no more than one half of the mother's total weight gain.

The other half, which is maternal weight gain, is mostly fluid. The mother's total circulating blood volume increases by about forty percent. If she usually has eight pints of blood circulating, this increases to nearly twelve pints. With one pint of blood roughly the equivalent of one pound, this extra blood adds at least four pounds to her weight.

The extra blood is not quite the same as her normal blood. It is predominantly plasma—the adjustable component of blood—rather than red blood cells. Plasma helps in regulating body temperature, so if an adult is exposed to very high temperatures, for instance, the plasma volume of his blood increases to accommodate the change and keep him from "burning up." Because the unborn baby has no external skin surface of his own to regulate his temperature, his mother must be equipped to do the temperature regulation necessary for them both.

This increase in fluid volume shows up in a number of ways that affect both how the mother feels and looks. Her body maintains a slightly higher temperature throughout pregnancy. It is more moist, and thus her skin takes on the "wet pink" look which we associate with pregnant women. Since she has more fluid to transport, there is more strain on the superficial veins of her legs, and there is a possibility of varicose veins. Because of this, mothers are asked to rest at least one hour each day during their pregnancy—with their feet propped up high. This is actually a fine time to catch up on knitting or reading "at doctor's orders."

There is also a noticeable change in the mother's body contours, which is due partly to the enlarging womb and partly to the increased blood volume. This gives a pleasing roundness to her face, neck, arms, and ankles.

Lethargy and nausea (referred to as morning sickness though not confined to the morning) are very common subjective symptoms of early pregnancy, and are often accompanied by a wan look, but with the fluid accumulation, after the third month many thin women come to look their roundest and prettiest.

Occasionally pregnant women, brunettes more commonly than blondes, develop a slightly blotchy pigmentation to their facial skin, which appears in the form of freckles, spots, or patches of darker color. This dark cast can be quite attractive on some women, while it gives others a dusty, dirty look. In either case it is a temporary, reversible condition that will disappear when the baby is born.

The greatest single cause of difficulty during labor and birth is a gross weight gain. Yet, because of the changes in the body's metabolism, many women experience a perverted appetite (medically known as pica) and have an excessive craving for odd foods, or too much food. This is a part of pregnancy where self-control is extremely important. For the sake of her own health the mother must make every effort to curb an inordinate appetite. Indulgence at this time may result in serious complications at delivery.

Women who are accustomed to a high protein diet are lucky, since fair quantities of lean meat, fish, eggs, cheese, fruits, and leafy vegetables can be consumed without risking a great weight gain.

Milk, while required in the diet of a pregnant woman, should not be taken in any greater quantity than ordinarily. Full milk is primarily a baby food and contains proteins, carbohydrates, and fats in roughly equal proportions, so necessary for the rapid growth of children.

Excessive milk taken in pregnancy will lead to obesity in the mother and do nothing for the child. We know that the child's actual caloric needs during pregnancy are not more than his mother's body can provide even when she is almost starving. In occupied countries during the war many pregnant women became mere skin-and-bone, yet their babies were born with a normal average birth weight. In some Arabic states where extreme obesity has become a beauty cult, women have grown to a stage where they could barely support themselves when standing, and the weight was gained simply by drinking large volumes of milk.

Reluctant to relinquish their former strong advocacy of milk, some dieticians have claimed that milk is required in pregnancy to provide calcium to build strong bones and teeth in the baby. In actual fact there is a vast store of calcium in the normal maternal body, and the requirements of baby's bones, only partly calcified at birth, and teeth, still minute and beneath the gums, are easily met. Although anybody's teeth may decay and require extraction for want of adequate dental care, pregnancy does not precipitate loss of teeth. Sound teeth are the most durable part of our bodies and have been known to last in the ground for millennia.

Women who love food should not delude themselves with the idea that fat weight gained in pregnancy will soon be run off when there is a baby to look after. Exercise does not reduce weight readily. Most people would need to walk about forty miles to lose one pound of fat weight from their bodies. In a recent study of overweight middle-aged English women it was found that seventy-five percent had first become obese during one of their pregnancies. Curtailing fat-producing foods in no way limits the size of the baby, and excessive weight will increase risk at birth.

On no account should the mother attempt to control her weight by cutting down on her fluid intake. The rule of thumb for a healthy pregnancy is to eat for one, but drink for two. During certain periods in pregnancy the fluid requirement for the mother is doubled. More fluid is lost from the body because in middle and late pregnancy breathing is more rapid. This increased breathing is caused by hormones produced by the conceptus, with the result that the mother breathes more than vigorously enough for two. The air we breathe out from our lungs is very damp and constitutes unavoidable loss of water. It is common for a woman to feel warm in pregnancy because of her temporary internal central heating plant, her baby. But a body must not become overheated, and the most effective way to dispose of body heat is through the skin surface. Sweating constitutes quite a large fluid loss, particularly in hot weather. The mechanism used by nature has been imitated in those canvas water bags that are hung on the bumpers of cars for desert travel. Water seeps through the surface of the bag and, as it evaporates, draws heat from the contents of the bag.

There is no known condition in pregnancy where reduction of fluid is indicated. Frequent trips to the toilet are one of the unalterable facts of pregnancy and are due to the general increased turnover of body water. However, if this frequency is accompanied by pain or irritation it should be reported to the doctor, since infection of the urinary tract is a reasonably frequent concomitant of the distortion of abdominal organs as the uterus enlarges.

Increased fluid intake is also required to sustain the

general increase in body fluid and circulating blood. Some dilution of red cells within the blood occurs, producing an apparent anemia. However, it is not safe to assume that a low blood count in pregnancy is merely due to this dilution. Since women only just make up the iron lost monthly with menstruation—even though they are on a good diet—they rarely build up a reserve supply. A true anemia is very common in pregnancy, and supplemental iron should always be taken. The only other supplement really necessary for women who eat a balanced diet is fluoride, and this only in parts of the country where the soil is deficient in fluoride.

While the obstetrician will always view weight accumulation above accepted limits with professional alarm, he will also be concerned about the woman who gains very little weight in pregnancy; this may indicate either poor placental function and hormone production in the baby or ill health in the mother.

We can only guess at "perfect" weights, since each person has his own ideal weight, depending on his body structure. A woman tends to be at her ideal weight on her wedding day, and she can use that weight as a goal throughout her pregnancies. When carrying one baby, the total weight gain should not exceed from twenty to thirty pounds. The one thing that will tell the truth about weight is the scale. If it shows too rapid a gain, a woman is eating too much—and must stop.

No one who is overweight can have ideal posture. Our skeletal structure depends on mechanics, just as a good bridge has stresses in the right places. If a woman stands badly, and the stresses on bones are in the wrong places, the entire mechanism is thrown out of gear. To find her own ideal posture, she should stand before a full-length mirror, naked or in a bathing suit. There should be a perpendicular line from the mastoid bone, behind her ear, down to the ankle bone.

One of our obstetrical headaches is that so many women in the Western world tend to slump over when they are pregnant. It is not only bad for the body, but it looks ugly. Tahitian women manage to look graceful throughout their pregnancies because they are accustomed to standing—and walking—tall. In order to balance the forward thrust of the pregnant uterus, the shoulders should be pulled high rather than back. Since high-heeled shoes tend to throw the body even further forward, low heels should be worn the majority of the time. Many painful orthopedic troubles that arise during and after pregnancy are directly traceable to the combination of poor posture and lack of adequate exercise. A doctor who heads one of the large maternity hospitals in the United States commented recently that "if every maternity hospital had an adjoining golf course, we would have less problems after."

It is important to keep up normal daily activities so that the muscles remain strong and the joints mobile. Swimming is perfectly safe. A daily walk is a must. A woman should continue any sport which she enjoys as long as she feels happy about playing it. What muscle tone and suppleness she can maintain throughout pregnancy will serve her well during labor and birth, and will facilitate and shorten the period of recovery afterward.

Since the baby is encapsulated in a bag of fluid and protected by the closed neck of the womb, no harm can be done to him from intercourse during pregnancy, up until the last month before birth. This is normal and healthy from both the physical and emotional points of view. During pregnancy the mother especially needs to be reassured of her husband's love and feel close to him. Practically, the physical act of love maintains her suppleness as well as peace of mind and aids in averting a period of stiffness and soreness following the birth.

The rate of weight gain during the middle phase of pregnancy begins to slow down in the seventh to the ninth month. Then, in the last, "winding down" phase after the baby is born, the mother should lose all the weight that she gained as a direct result of pregnancy. First there is the expulsion of the baby, his bag of waters and placenta. Then, less dramatically, there is a reduction of the mother's blood volume and body fluid, and a gradual reduction in the size of the womb, birth passages, and abdominal wall. Ideally, she should match her pre-pregnancy weight about two months after the baby is born. Occasionally women store an excess of fluid during pregnancy—but this fluid does not remain in her body once the baby has been delivered.

Breasts enlarge, in varying degrees, throughout pregnancy, although this accounts for no more than two pounds of the mother's total weight increase. Some women who normally have quite small breasts are so delighted with their voluptuous new contours that they are disappointed when the breasts eventually go back to the size they were before pregnancy.

The breasts should receive attention from the time that they first begin to enlarge. A good supporting maternity brassiere should be worn during pregnancy, and used both day and night during breast-feeding. As soon as any discharge appears, which usually does not occur until the last months of pregnancy, the breasts should be gently bathed each day, dried, and then rubbed with a little lanolin or olive oil. Flattened or inverted nipples require no special treatment, and rarely affect breast-feeding, since the milk flow comes from the pressure of the baby's mouth on the area surrounding the nipple, rather than from the nipple itself. Some women's breasts sag considerably with the extra weight during pregnancy, but this has to do with the type of body rather than with the supply of milk. When the extra weight load is gone, the breasts will regain the same contour they had before pregnancy.

The question of whether the mother wishes to breast-feed her baby or not is one that only she can answer. Breast feeding is actually such an intimate part of our human life cycle that our reaction to the question reflects our approach to life. The proportion of women who breast-feed their babies is not so much a measure of our economics or our sophistication as it is of our confidence and joy in motherhood.

The greatest problem in breast feeding in the Western world is not physiological, but simply women's attitudes toward their own reproductive function. Failure to understand their nature has reduced the number of women who successfully breast-feed their babies to less than one in every two.

Part of this problem is due to a lack of education about our own humanity. At school we are taught the life cycles of the butterfly and the moth, but never the natural life cycle of the human being. Most of us can trace the butterfly from the egg through the larval stage, to the chrysalis, and finally to the insect, beautiful in its maturity, but what can we say about our own natural functions as human male and female? Pregnancy presents an appropriate time to pause and take a look at what we actually are.

Ideally, the human life cycle would read something like this:

Two young creatures, in full physical maturity, both able to satisfy their physical hunger with food and their fatigue with sleep, meet and are emotionally drawn to one another. At first nearness delights them, then close physical contact. They become partners, and in complete emotional and physical union they achieve ecstasy of the spirit. The female becomes overwhelmed with the desire to consummate this ecstasy in new life. In time new life begins. Commencing as a single cell, the new being settles to grow in the body of the female. Through her body it receives nourishment, while she, in turn, is sustained by the efforts of her partner.

The first stage of this new life, the stage of complete dependence, lasts about one year—from the conception through early infancy. Like the full year, the new life has its seasons. The first, spring, is the metamorphosis from a single cell into a tiny creature a few inches long, who, like Alice, swims freely in a pool of tears of his own making. The next, summer, is the one of rapid growth, faster than he will again know within his lifetime.

By autumn there is a ripening-off process as the new life fills up the space he lives in and begins preparing himself for survival in the outside world. A new method of feeding develops, and the unborn creature practices this new art by sucking his own thumb, and swallowing some of the fluid that surrounds him.

As the winter season draws near, intermittent pressure changes squeeze the new life wholly, and line him up for the next step in the cycle, like a ship bracing itself to meet the storm. Winter is ushered in with a violent storm which gains momentum, wave upon wave, driving the little creature mercilessly against a restricting orifice, forcing it gradually to open, until, finally freed, he can be squeezed out,

taut, and protesting, to freedom. The mother, who anticipated the storm, takes comfort and courage from her partner,
and when the thrill of the storm has passed, she experiences
a marvelous peace. She, in turn, comforts the new life beside
her, by holding him in her arms and offering him her breast.

It is unfortunate that the human life cycle we have just
described, which is as beautiful and simple in its natural
function as any form of life, is so often grievously
distorted. Husbands are cut off from their wives' confidence in pregnancy and labor. Newborn babies are kept
away from their mothers during the first days when they
most need them. Breast feeding is discouraged, with argu-
ments that range from cosmetic values to overworked
hospital staffs who simply don't want to be bothered with
bringing the newborn babies to their mothers for their
feedings.

There are actually few valid reasons for not breast-feeding a baby. It represents the completion of pregnancy—
the mother finishes the job she started. Today, in no more
than two or three cases in each hundred pregnancies is a
mother physically incapable of breast-feeding her child.
Mastitis, infection of the breasts, which at one time destroyed breast tissue, can now be controlled with anti-
biotics. Retained parts of the placenta and profound anemia will interfere with the flow of breast milk, but doctors
can now deal effectively with each of these conditions.
Cracked nipples rarely occur if the babies are fed when
they are hungry and only at times when the breast milk
is flowing freely.

The mother who wishes to breast-feed her baby should
certainly plan to do so. She has the right to insist on
this, and her request cannot be denied. Breast feeding
brings both physical and psychological rewards. Through

the natural laws that adjust supply to demand, the mother who breast-feeds her baby usually avoids painful engorgement following the birth. For whether she plans to feed her baby or not, her breasts prepare for it, and if she does not let the baby suckle the milk that is there, she will experience painful swelling of breast tissue and blood vessels each time the milk is flowing.

On a purely practical level, it is much easier to nurse the newborn baby, provided a woman has a good milk supply, than to be constantly worrying about formulas and bottles and sterilization—especially during those first few weeks when the baby demands a feeding six or seven times within each twenty-four hours.

On the psychological level, the mother is rewarded with the confidence that she is able to provide her baby's most pressing need. She is helping him to settle peacefully into his new environment.

Breast feeding provides the newborn with a type of feeding for which he has been preparing himself in the womb. Even more important, it gives him his initial introduction to the strange new world of emotion. His first three interpreted emotional experiences relate to first feeding: He feels hunger distress, then the comfort of the breast, and finally the satisfaction from nourishment. Ideally these first three emotions should involve the baby's own mother. Breast feeding provides the perfect opportunity for this vital interchange between the baby and the mother.

chapter three

THE FETUS AS
AN INDIVIDUAL

The unborn baby is an active, lively, independent human being long before his mother feels his presence. By the third month of pregnancy he has developed from the first single cell of life into a perfectly formed little creature about the size of his father's thumb. He has survived the early critical stage when his organs were forming and he is now firmly entrenched, immune to almost anything, and extremely difficult to dislodge.

More than any living species, this tiny Tom Thumb of a human being dominates his environment. At three months, he has succeeded in taking over his mother's body and has altered it to suit his own needs. The milieu in which he lives—his umbilical cord, the placenta, and the amniotic sac (bag of waters)—belong to him rather than to his mother, since they have all developed from the original cell. At this stage his mother could have her ovaries removed, or be unconscious from an injury, and her baby would go right on developing inside her, since he manufactures quite enough hormones to sustain the pregnancy for them both.

Inside the body of the independent little creature, his

pea-sized heart is pumping blood around the minute vessels which supply the limbs, organs, and brain. Then, the blood moves on through a long extension of his own vessels, which, leaving at the navel, course out through his lifeline, the umbilical cord, to the placenta—that way station for the absorption of food and discharge of waste through his mother's body.

The baby's blood vessels break up into minute branches in the placenta, which is like a root system, drawing nourishment from the mother's blood stream. Neither the cord nor the placenta is connected to the mother in any way. They are a distinct part of the baby which he will discard at birth. The blood that passes along the cord and the placenta is his blood, pulsed by his own tiny heart. The blood of the mother and baby do not mix. The placenta serves as a fairly perfect barrier between the two blood streams, and only tiny amounts of the baby's blood ever escape into the mother's circulatory system.

Only now are we beginning to understand the marvels of the placenta. It was long thought that this complex and mysterious organ was part of the mother. Actually it belongs to the baby, and establishes itself in the mother's body. While it appears to be little more than an extensive network of blood vessels, the placenta is capable of performing the tasks of kidney, intestines, liver, endocrine glands, and lungs. It works harmoniously with the growing requirements of the developing fetus, so that some functions that are at first carried out by the placenta are adopted by fetal organs as term approaches. Through it the baby receives both nutrients and oxygen from the mother's blood stream, and exchanges carbon dioxide and wastes. Immune bodies can cross the placenta from the maternal circulation to the baby, giving him immunity, which will last for several months following birth, to diseases to which the mother is immune. This provides the newborn a standby until he has time to develop strength to meet disease.

It is through the multiple functions of the marvelous placenta that the tiny parasite of a fetus is able to "put a boss in the factory" and take over his mother's body for his own purposes. Without the placenta, the mother-host would not tolerate such an invasion. She would reject her baby as a homograft, the same as if we tried to graft a piece of skin from another individual onto her own. If the skin of her own newborn baby were grafted onto her body, she would reject it. Yet the action of this complex and amazing machine enables the fetus to live out his entire growing period within her body, undisturbed.

The unborn baby is an aquatic animal—a sort of combination astronaut and underwater swimmer—who lives in a balloon of fluid. The amniotic fluid, which at this stage completely surrounds him, acts as a shock absorber and provides a constant temperature. Falls or knocks sustained by his mother affect him little. And, as the astronaut, he has the further advantage of "weightlessness" with little gravitational draw. Today we are studying the unborn human astronaut to gain knowledge for adult space missions. It was found that when adult astronauts experienced the weightless state in space travel, one of the problems they encountered was diuresis, the passing of large quantities of urine. This problem in "space plumbing" is handled swiftly and efficiently by the unborn, who simply sends waste along through the placenta to his mother to get rid of for him and uses the fluid from his bladder to replenish his "bath water." No such convenience has yet been discovered to care for our adult space travelers.

Because the fetus is benignly protected, warmed, and nourished within the womb, it was long thought that the unborn must have the nature of a plant, static in habit, and growing only in size. Recently, through modern techniques of diagnosing and treating the unborn baby, we have discovered that little could be further from the truth. The balloon of fluid is at first large in proportion to the tiny body, and the unborn of three months is buoyant and active. His movements to and fro, round and around, up and down, have the wonderfully relaxed grace which we see in films of life under water. Although he is so small —a scant three inches long—that only rarely is a mother aware of his activities, he is really very busy, swimming around in his own private space capsule.

It is unfortunate that we only see our little Tom Thumbs in an aborted state, removed from their watery environment. Like a sea anemone snatched from its rocky pool, their magical beauty is instantly lost and they are apt to appear misshapen and shriveled. The fluid that surrounds the human fetus at three, four, five, and six months is essential to both its growth and its grace. The unborn's structure at this early stage is highly liquid, and although his organs have developed, he does not have the same relative bodily proportions that a newborn baby has. The head, housing the miraculous brain, is quite large in proportion to the remainder of the body, and the limbs are still relatively small. Within his watery world, however (where we have been able to observe him in his natural state through a sort of closed-circuit x-ray television set), he is quite beautiful, perfect in his fashion, active and graceful. He is neither a quiescent vegetable nor a witless tadpole, as some have conceived him to be in the past, but rather a tiny human being, as independent as though he were lying in a crib with a blanket wrapped around him instead of his mother.

Mothers frequently worry that their unborn babies, in their gyrations, may tangle themselves in their umbilical cords and strangle. Most cords average around twenty inches in length, although they have been known to be as long as one hundred. With this much "rope" present in his capsule, it is quite common for the baby, in his restless movements, to get his cord wrapped around his body or his neck. However, in the intra-uterine stage, the cord is filled with blood that is flowing through it at a high rate —as much as a half a pint per minute. Under this high flow rate, the cord is at all times relatively rigid, stiff, and erectile, much like a garden hose under a full pressure flow of water. When the unborn baby encounters his cord —which he frequently does—he can usually manage to disengage himself quite easily since it is not sufficiently flexible to knot. If the cord is long enough to make some sort of loop, it is also too long to pull the loop tight. It is only in the final moments of delivery, when the cord has lost the flow of blood which keeps it stiff, that the baby might entangle himself with some danger, since the cord is then capable of knotting. But by then the attending obstetrician can take care of the emergency and assist the baby. The cord that we see following birth bears little resemblance to its condition in the uterus, since, without its burden of blood, it becomes slack and ropelike.

Contrary to much that has been written in the past by both doctors and poets, the womb is neither dark nor silent. Although the development of sight in the unborn is limited by lack of bright light, the baby's eyes do open

THE DEVELOPMENT OF THE FETUS

1

Three weeks *After fertilization, embryo reaches 1/12 of an inch long, and about 1/6 inch wide. Already the backbone is forming, and the spinal canal, with 5 or 6 vertebrae laid down.*

2

Fourth week *The head is forming, the heart is visible. All of the backbone is now laid down and the spinal canal is closed over. The beginnings of arms and legs are visible, as well as the depressions beneath the skin where the eyes will appear.*

3

Fifth week *The chest and abdomen are formed, and the fingers and toes are beginning to take shape. By now the eyes are clearly perceptible. The embryo is about 1/2 inch long.*

4

Sixth week *The ears are forming and the facial features are becoming visible.*

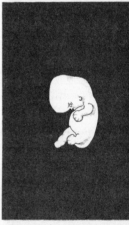

5

Seventh and Eighth weeks *(Two Months) Now the face is completely formed. The arms, legs, hands, feet, toes and fingers are partially formed. The fetus is over one inch in length and weighs two or three grams.*

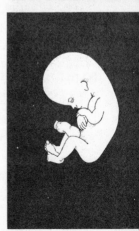

6

Third month   *The arms, legs, feet, toes,
hands and ears are fully formed. Nails beginning
to appear, and external genital organs beginning
to show differences in shape. The fetus is now
a full three inches long and weighs an ounce.*

7

Fourth month   *Eyebrows and eyelashes
appear. Genital organs show sex of infant.
Weight: 6 ounces.*

8

Fifth month   *Hair beginning to appear on
head. Now weighs about one pound and is
a foot long.*

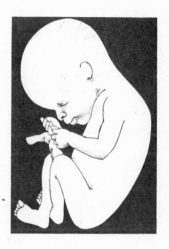

9

Sixth month   *Hair on head. Eyes open.
Two pounds in weight.*

10

Seventh month   *Child born at this age
has a good chance of survival. Weight is around
3 pounds—or over.*

11

Eighth month   *Child is 18 inches long
and weighs over five pounds. Has a 90% chance of
survival if born now.*

12

Ninth month   *Full-term baby has smooth
skin, 1-inch-long head hair, long fingernails and
toenails. Average length: 20 inches,
weight: 7 pounds.*

and shut in the womb, and he is able to see. At birth his eyes will be nearly adult size, and he will be able to distinguish between light and shadow. Since the womb remains dimly lit, however, even when his mother stands unclothed in sunlight, the baby's visual stimuli are confined to the rods of the retina—that part of the eye which we use to see at night and to distinguish brightness rather than detail. As a result the newborn baby, while by no means blind, does interpret brightness long before he can interpret shape, and he will invariably reach for the shiniest toy before its shape has any meaning for him.

Young parents are frequently disappointed because their newborn babies possess such a blank, uncomprehending stare. They do not "talk" with their eyes and faces and show emotion, as adults have learned to do. But a newly born baby needs several weeks of experience in the brightly lit outside world to learn to distinguish shapes and details. And then, only through imitating the adult faces that keep peering at him, does he finally associate shapes with the expression of emotion.

Since the baby's nose remains under water until his birth, the unborn does not have much opportunity to develop his sense of smell. Besides, there is little stimulus within the amniotic sac, where everything smells the same. In my own experience, I have noticed that babies do not seem to develop a noticeable sense of smell until they reach nine or ten months of age. A very young baby, for example, will eat almost anything—vegetables, eggs, or bacon, it seems to make little difference—although that very same food may prove an anathema to him six months later and he will violently reject it. This is because the sense of taste depends, to a very great extent, upon the sense of smell—as any of us will realize when we have a head cold and "everything tastes the same." As the new-born baby's sense of smell improves, he becomes far more selective about what he will eat.

The unborn baby is capable of learning at a very fast rate. But his learning within the uterus is conditioned and limited by the stimuli that reach his brain. While the womb presents rather restricted stimuli for the development of both sight and smell, there are far more stimuli for the development of the unborn's sense of hearing. The womb, we have found, is an extremely noisy place. The unborn is exposed to a multiplicity of sounds that range from his mother's heartbeat and her voice to outside street noises. Especially if his mother has not gotten too plump, a great many outside noises come through to the unborn baby quite clearly: auto crashes, sonic booms, music. And the rumblings of his mother's bowel and her intestines are constantly with him. If she should drink a glass of champagne or a bottle of beer, the sounds, to her unborn baby, would be something akin to rockets being shot off all around. A child who sleeps sixteen to twenty hours out of each twenty-four, as both the unborn and the new-born baby do, learns very rapidly in his waking moments. In only a few weeks following his birth, the baby will be able to identify and distinguish his mother by the sounds that she makes.

One of the newer devices that is now being tested and used in some hospital nurseries to reassure and comfort the newborn babies is a machine, developed in Japan, which simulates the rhythmic dub-dub-dub sound of the mother's heartbeat to which the infant was accustomed in the womb. The machine records an actual human heartbeat and plays it through a loudspeaker system into the nursery where all the babies can hear it. Apparently this is very soothing to small babies; for the adult who first walks into a nursery and hears the amplified, all-pervading heartbeat, it is an eerie experience, reminiscent of an avant-garde motion picture or a piece of science fiction. Mothers occasionally try the same idea on their newborn babies (and on puppies who cry for their mothers) by wrapping an alarm clock in a soft woolen covering to muffle the tick so that it resembles the thud of the human heart, and then put it in the crib or nearby where the baby can hear it.

One of the most insidious of the old wives' tales designed to frighten young mothers is that their emotional state will have an adverse influence on their unborn babies. Someone invariably tells the young woman during her first pregnancy that if she is bad-tempered or nervous, or screams a lot, this state of emotion will "mark" her child, or predispose it to an unhappy life. In late pregnancy, after they are familiar with their baby's movements, many mothers will describe hearing a loud or unpleasant sound and feeling their baby jump within the womb in reaction to it. It is true, as the poets maintain, that the unborn baby does "leap in its mother's womb," but he does not leap because he is emotionally disturbed. The baby's reaction to loud noise is sheer instinct—one of the few instincts, in fact, which the human being has left. Similarly, when someone claps his hands loudly or stamps on the floor, a newborn automatically jumps or starts. When the unborn jumps in reaction to a loud noise, whether it was made by his own mother's scream or a truck trundling by, it is not because he has an emotional response to the sound. Emotion would require that the baby relate the sound to some experience. The sound means nothing because he has nothing unpleasant to associate it with. The small child soon learns that when his mother's voice rises in a certain way he is probably due for a smack on the bottom—and he recoils. His reaction is emotional, because he anticipates what experience has led him to expect.

But to the unborn baby loud noises are just loud noises. The absence of fear or other emotion in a baby's reaction to an external situation was proved quite vividly to us when we were demonstrating a fetal electrocardiogram at our hospital. The mother was lying on a table in the delivery room; a microphone on her abdomen was picking up the electrical recordings of her baby's heartbeat, which then appeared charted in a graph on a revolving drum. A prominent surgeon from the British Medical Research Council came in to watch. The mother was very shy and modest, and when she saw this impressive looking VIP come over to the table where she was lying to speak to her, she became very agitated and embarrassed. The recording that we were watching of the baby's heartbeat dropped at the moment he entered, then accelerated violently—just as though her unborn child were enduring her embarrassment and confusion with her. What had actually happened, however, was that when the mother became upset and frightened, adrenaline was released into her blood stream and passed through the placenta into her baby's body. The baby thereupon experienced the physical response to his mother's emotion—without first having experienced the emotion. Her confusion and fright were no more than a slight physical discomfort for her unborn child.

It is ridiculous and unhealthy to assume that a woman must restrain her emotions because she is carrying a baby. When an expectant mother laughs, rages, weeps, or shouts, it has about the same effect on her unborn baby as if she dropped a saucepan. I think we would become pitiful objects if we tried too hard to stay always in one gear.

The unborn does react to his mother's tempo and movement because this relates to something he comprehends: his own physical comfort. He is quite aware of the difference in the times when his mother is rushing about to get chores and errands done, and when she is walking rhythmically and quietly, giving him a nice ride, rather like the carriage stroll through the shady park he will have after he is born. Even though he does not have to contend with gravity, the vibrations outside his space capsule get through to him. And when he's in a mood for a quiet sleep and his mother joggles him about, he is apt to make his protest known. After the fifth or sixth month, when the unborn baby is large enough to be clearly felt by his mother, she may notice that at the times she is dashing around, she is liable to get a sharp kick of protest from her unborn baby.

For the harried mother it may sometimes seem that her newborn's desires are quite arbitrary and perverse. At dinner time, for instance, when the mother is most active, trying to get supper cooked and on the table for her husband and other children, the unborn would usually much prefer a nice, quiet nap. But he doesn't stand much chance with all that bouncing around his mother gives him as she trots back and forth from the stove to the dining table. She probably is too busy to notice if he does express himself with a sharp jab or kick. But later he has a fine chance, after he is born, to get even with her. Just when she most wishes the new baby would stay asleep and be quiet so that she can be free to serve supper to the rest of the family, the baby awakes. He has been conditioned that this is precisely the time of day when he always got the worst jouncing while he was in the womb. Therefore, he cries and complains until someone comes and picks him up and bounces him on his shoulder. I'm sure if a poll were taken it would be found that the majority of tiny babies are perversely at their very brightest and most demanding at around six o'clock.

The infant's awareness and adjustment— or lack of it —to his mother's movements and tempo, just as his awareness of the sound of his mother's voice, however, have to do with physical comfort rather than with any emotions on his part. His mother's dartings about do not predispose the baby to the same temperament, although he may very well have inherited some of the same on-the-go nature that his mother has. But he would have that inherited disposition whether she moved quickly or not.

The mother's emotional state most strongly affects her unborn child in that the way she behaves when pregnant is also liable to be the way she will behave after he is born. And it is in the first few days and weeks of her baby's life, immediately following his birth, that he will be most directly influenced by his mother's emotions.

chapter four

THE MOTHER FEELS
HER BABY

The unborn baby's growth between the third and seventh months of his intra-uterine life is rapid and unequal—faster than he will ever again grow within his lifetime. There may be as much as a twelve-inch increase in length. When you think what it would be like to have to let down the hem of a little girl's dress a full foot each four months, you realize that nature very wisely selected this time for the child's fastest growing period. As his limbs grow in size, the unborn's overall physical activity increases and becomes progressively more vigorous so that, after the fifth month, strong movements impinge on the front of the womb. These will be felt by the mother as knocks against her abdominal wall and at long last she will feel the "quickening," as the Bible calls it, within her, and know for certain that she is carrying a live child.

Some women feel their babies much more strongly than others do, depending on their own body fat and also upon the position of the placenta. If the placenta lies in the front of the mother's uterus, serving as a sort of buffer between the unborn and his mother's abdominal wall, she may feel her baby only slightly throughout her pregnancy. There have been women who never felt their babies at all. Others are not able to differentiate between what feels like a "slight gas pain" and the thrust of their baby's fist or elbow or foot. Occasionally women have reported feeling the first faint fluttering of their baby's movements as early as twelve weeks after conception, but the majority of women do not recognize and identify the sensation until the fifth month of pregnancy. The doctor usually recognizes fetal movement about the same time when he is listening with his stethoscope for fetal heartbeat and can hear movement.

Historically, "quickening" was supposed to delineate the time when the fetus became an independent human being possessed of a soul. Now, however, we know that, while he may have been too small to make his motions felt, the unborn baby is active and independent long before his mother feels him. His early movements, during the third, fourth, and fifth months, are subconscious acts, part of and essential to his overall growth. His strength of muscular action following his birth will be dependent upon the muscular power that he developed by his movements in the womb. The newborn baby is thus able to thrust or kick out—actions that he practiced in the uterus —yet has little power in his back or his neck muscles, since they were relatively immobilized by the cramped position he maintained in late intra-uterine life. The unborn's earliest movements are reflex in character, conditioned by his inherited temperament. From the fifth month on, however, some of his actions become consciously determined; and these are most frequently motivated by discomfort.

The time of quickening is often a worrisome time for anxious mothers. The women who look forward to it and then do not feel anything worry whether their baby is alive. Those who feel motion, and then feel it cease, worry that something may have gone wrong with the child. Usually by the sixth month their fears are alleviated, since by this time the unborn baby will be felt to move frequently each day. So long as the uterus remains globular and the unborn is small, he has considerable choice of position, putting his pillow wherever he wants to in his circular bed. He lies with his head up for a while, then tries it down, shifting to suit his fancy. He moves from the left side to the right. We have recorded babies turning completely around twice within two minutes' time.

With all this shifting about, the baby is very likely to poke his mother's abdominal wall so sharply with an elbow or knee that if she is watching she can see her abdomen distend in the spot he hits. It is an exciting sensation to watch the movement of a baby—only a few inches away, still unseen, but very much alive. Fathers frequently enjoy sharing this discovery. All one has to do is press the palms of both hands on the mother's abdomen and wait a few minutes. Soon one will be rewarded with an identifiable kick or nudge from the other side of the abdominal wall.

First babies often seem less lively than later ones because the uterus is usually less elastic; with a second child the uterus is more easily distended and provides the baby more room to roam around in. Also, fat women feel fetal movement much less than thin women do. A few grossly fat women have given birth to babies without ever knowing for certain that they were pregnant.

Before we developed reliable medical means of diagnosing the diseases of the unborn, it was often the mother who was first aware that something was wrong with her baby, because he had either stopped moving entirely, or was moving much more feebly than before. Now, however, we are generally able to anticipate trouble long before it has reached such a stage, through analyses of blood and urine, and if hemolytic disease is indicated, through examination of the amniotic fluid.

As the unborn occupies more and more of the available space within the enlarging womb, he has less room to wiggle around in, and his movements usually diminish within the final two months of pregnancy. His surrounding fluid also diminishes in proportion to his growth, and is eventually confined to the pockets that are left by the irregularities of his body surface. With no fluid bath left in which to stretch out full length, the baby curls up. As pregnancy progresses, the uterus changes from globular to an inverted pear-shape, so that the maximum space is now at the top of his capsule. His bed has elongated as has his own body.

The largest single part of the baby is his head. But when he lies curled up, as he does in late pregnancy, the area that is composed of his buttocks, thighs, legs, and feet all drawn up together is larger than his head. It is because of this distribution that we find that ninety-seven percent of all babies will lie in the head-down position in the uterus during late pregnancy. These babies are all born in the most usual and easy way—head first. Despite the loss of much of his surrounding fluid, the baby still exists in a weightless state so that gravity is no problem for him, and lying head down does not make him dizzy as it would us. On the contrary, the unborn baby selects this position because it is the most comfortable way he can lie in his limited space. The occasional unborn individual who is most comfortable, for reasons relating to the limitations of his mother's uterus or to his own construction, with his legs over his shoulders, will select the breech position. If a mother is curious as to what position a newborn was lying in while he was still in the womb, she should let him lie naked in a warm room until he falls asleep. If he has neither clothes nor sheets to restrict his subconscious movement, he will select his pre-birth position. While some doctors do try to turn babies who are lying in breech position to facilitate the delivery, we have found that, what with the unborn being as strong-minded as he is about his own comfort, it is really useless to attempt to change him. If he likes it best that way, his will dominates, and if the doctor turns him, the baby turns right back again.

In cases of multiple birth it is usual for the babies to appear in alternating positions: the first one will come head down, and the next will be a breech, etc., since they could not all lie the same way in the available uterine space. With twins, the one who pre-empts the most comfortable position and gets himself born first is likely to remain the dominant personality throughout life.

As we began to diagnose and treat the unborn baby as a patient, separate from his mother, the one predominant characteristic that we could rely on in all unborn babies —short of those so ill they were already moribund— was the baby's concern with his own comfort. The awareness of comfort and discomfort becomes a reality for the unborn baby as his body fills up the available uterine space and he is no longer floating free. While our little three-month fetus, suspended in his liquid balloon, had very little chance of being uncomfortable, the baby who has filled up his capsule begins to connect more and more frequently with the objects that lie outside it—just as a

ship near the shore strikes shoals. One of the most uncomfortable ledges that the unborn can encounter is his
mother's backbone. If he happens to be lying so that his
own backbone is across hers, there is little fleshy padding
between the two bony areas, and it feels to him as though
he were lying in a bed of rocks. If you've ever camped
out, and mistakenly placed your sleeping bag on a rocky
piece of ground, you know the feeling. If he has any choice
in the matter, the unborn will wriggle around until he can
get away from this highly disagreeable position. This is
the reason that late in pregnancy, when the mother is
tired and lies down on her back to sleep at night, her baby,
who has not yet been civilized into gallantry, is apt to
object. He kicks and turns and twists, and until he has
located a better napping ground for himself, his mother
has difficulty getting to sleep.

Doctors have learned to make use of this common trait
of the unborn when they are going to give a blood transfusion to an anemic baby suffering hemolytic disease
(which is done only when the anemia resulting from the
Rh factor is known to be critical). At one time the mother
was allowed to do as she pleased until time for the transfusion. But if she spent her time walking around her
room or visiting before coming into the operating theater,
her baby was wide awake, restless, and on the move. The
baby moved so much that the doctors had difficulty locat-
ing his abdominal wall. Now we have learned to sedate
the mother and bring her into the room at least twenty
minutes in advance and have her lie quietly on her back.
We know that wherever her baby is, once he has been
presented with this "bed of rocks" from his mother's backbone, he will disengage his own back and turn on his side,
either to the right or to the left. It really makes no dif-

ference to the surgeon which way his unseen patient chooses to turn; in either case, the unborn presents a flank, which provides the ideal operating target for fetal transfusion.

Another rule which was necessitated by what we learned to expect in unborn behavior, was that no visiting doctor is allowed any last-moment pokes or prods or listening with a stethoscope. This was put into effect after a visiting doctor laid a heavy microphone over a baby who was about to be transfused to listen to the fetal heartbeat —and the little patient became so indignant at this extra weight that he squirmed out of position and it took another twenty minutes to coax him back again.

Doctors who want to take a sample of the unborn's fluid in late pregnancy have learned that they can rely on the baby's spirited reaction to discomfort. By the time the baby is eight or nine months old, the biggest pool of fluid fills the indentations around his chin and neck. If the baby is lying in such a fashion that access to this pool with a needle is difficult, the surgeon simply presses his knuckles firmly against the unborn's body. Invariably the baby, even the sick baby, wiggles into another position in protest.

As soon as awareness develops in the unborn baby's brain, this consciousness of comfort and discomfort becomes increasingly important, and he soon exerts what we recognize as an arbitrary and extraordinarily strong will. Often this turns into a contest between himself and his mother. So long as she is up and about, with the womb slung forward like a comfortable hammock, her baby, even in late pregnancy when his quarters are quite cramped, can doze peacefully, swinging along as though she were taking him for a quiet stroller ride. But when she tires and decides to lie down, his comfortable hammock abruptly tilts him back onto her rocky backbone. Besides feeling his squirms of protest, the mother may also experience "heartburn" if the uterus tilting back onto her stomach forces acid up into the esophagus. The only thing to do, which is the same thing she will do for her newborn after his feedings, is to prop herself up—a difficult position for sleeping. It is often so difficult to sleep in late pregnancy that mothers understandably feel that the day will never come when this willful little body will get himself born.

Traditionally the final months of pregnancy have been designated as the "period of waiting." The fetus at this stage was once considered to be safe, secure, blind, growing quietly as a cabbage. On the contrary, we have found that he moves just as much as his cramped quarters allow. Some babies find room to kick in right up to the moment of birth. In addition to all this exercise to strengthen his muscles, the unborn in late pregnancy is busy practicing and perfecting the arts in his limited command which will tend to insure his survival once he reaches the outside world.

chapter five

THE FETUS PRACTICES
FOR BIRTH

A century ago a newborn infant's ability to suck and swallow would have determined his chances of survival, since his ability to feed properly at birth would dictate whether he would be a healthy baby or suffer acute undernourishment. The problem today is somewhat modified since we have learned medically how to feed the unskilled infant. But there is still no doubt that the baby who is adept and experienced at getting food through his mouth has a head start at both nourishment and the experience of pleasure.

Unless their swallowing apparatus is physiologically underdeveloped or restricted, all unborn babies learn to some degree how to suck and swallow while they are still in the womb, where they practice drinking their surrounding fluid. Some are better than others.

We have evidence, through x-rays, that the unborn baby is drinking his own fluid in small quantities by the time he is fourteen weeks old. He is already, at that very early stage of his existence, practicing the arts of sucking and swallowing which will insure his survival when he is born. Drinking his fluid gives the unborn baby something more than mere exercise. Analysis reveals that the fluid contains both protein and sugar and so has a small caloric content. Individual babies vary in how much fluid they drink. The very active ones will drink as much as six to eight pints of fluid per day by their eighth or ninth month. This averages five ounces per hour and is the caloric equivalent of three and a half ounces of milk per day. Some babies, because their esophagus is blocked, are unable to drink, and these babies are smaller than average at birth.

Even as the baby grows and fills up the uterine space, fluid is always present, no matter how much he drinks, since it constantly replaces itself. Most of the fluid is secreted by the fetal kidney, which at this stage does not function as an excretory organ but simply pours forth fluid, as does the kidney of an astronaut. It is also thought that some of the fluid is contributed by the fetal lung. The fetal skin, which has a very dense sweat gland population, also regularly pours forth fluid in the relatively hot, damp environment of the uterus. In spite of the baby's size, there are always pockets of fluid available, particularly in the crevices around his face.

The mouth is the part of the unborn baby's anatomy with which he is most familiar, both through instinctive sucking and through constant practice. His suckling instinct is abetted by habitual practice at swallowing, so that when he reaches term the baby is a master at the art of drinking. If he is an especially active baby he may even have indicated a characteristic tendency to overindulgence.

During my first pregnancy, I became quite concerned about odd rhythmic jerks within the womb which appeared to be distressingly like convulsions. When I asked

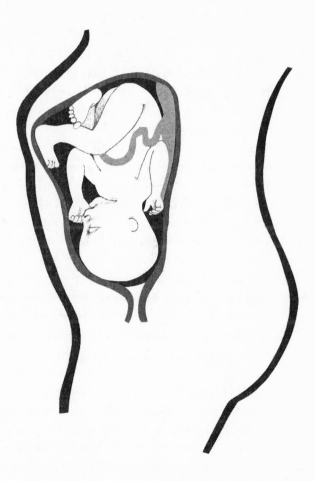

*The mouth will be very important in the
newborn period, and a baby learns to use it long
before birth, learning to suck, swallow and
explore with it. Note also that the uterus is
quite soft when relaxed and readily pushed aside
when the baby stretches.*

my husband (who is an obstetrician) to listen to the strange interior sounds, he did so for a moment or two, and then burst out laughing. "That baby is gulping his food and he's got hiccoughs," he told me. "I will make you a bet right now that when he is born he will have an inclination to eat too much, too fast." My eldest son, who is now ten years old, often eats so heartily that he has to lie down and rest following meals. And as a small baby he was very prone to hiccoughs.

The unborn finds his mouth with his hands quite early, and many x-rays show unborn babies of various ages sucking their thumbs. While this was once considered a bad habit because it was thought that thumb-sucking might alter the shape of a child's mouth, the most recent medical evidence, gathered by a group of British doctors and dentists, concludes that the habit is actually quite harmless and it has no effect on the shape of the mouth. Babies are apt to suck their thumbs *because* of the shape of their mouths, rather than altering their mouths by sucking their thumbs. Again, as is true of so much of fetal and newborn behavior, it is a question of comfort. If thumb-sucking is comfortable, then the baby will do it.

Much of what we have recently learned about the behavior of the unborn baby has evolved from our work in saving babies who might otherwise have a very limited chance of survival, because of the Rh factor, when their blood is not compatible with their mother's blood and they develop acute anemia. This condition rarely becomes evident until the final two months of pregnancy, usually around the thirtieth week. While the RH factor involves a small percent of babies, some of the diagnostic techniques that we have learned for that disease apply to other problems of the unborn; and someday we will be able to accurately diagnose and treat diseases that now remain undetected until the baby's birth.

Since it is the baby himself who is the patient and who can best tell the condition of the pregnancy, doctors have had to learn means of winning the co-operation of their small, invisible, but very lively and determined patients. The three factors that have enabled doctors to get acquainted with and treat their unborn patients, separate from the mother who surrounds them, are, first, that the predominant desire is for comfort; second, that the baby swallows much of his surrounding fluid; and third, that, just as any other human being, the unborn baby is quite aware of pain.

The suck-and-swallow factor is valuable for purposes of x-ray. If a transfusion is indicated, for example, the doctors inject dye into the amniotic sac and then take x-rays. The dye outlines the entire uterine contents so that they stand out as clearly as a charcoal sketch and can be checked for malformations. This dyed fluid is soon eliminated, by way of the placenta, through the mother. The doctors, however, have learned that before the dyed fluid is all drained out, the busily suckling unborn will have managed to swallow some of it. This fluid lodges in his own bowel, which does not empty until after he is born. From then on, the unborn's bowel remains a clearly labeled area of his body for all future x-ray—presenting a clear outline that is much easier to read, and serves as a far better target for transfusion than the outline of the fetal skeleton. By being able to accurately determine the precise limits of the baby's bowel, the surgeon who transfuses the baby can avoid a possible puncture of the liver which, in babies suffering acute anemia, is apt to be considerably enlarged.

When doctors first began invading the sanctuary of the womb, they did not know that the unborn baby would react to pain in the same fashion as a child would. But they soon learned that he does. By no means a "vegetable" as he has so often been pictured, the unborn knows perfectly well when he has been hurt, and he will protest it just as violently as would a baby lying in a crib. When the unborn "hurts" he reacts all over, just as the newborn baby does, by flaying out his tiny arms, wriggling his entire body, and crying. Although the watery environment in which he lives presents small opportunity for crying, which does require air, the unborn knows how to cry, and given a chance to do so, he will. A doctor who practices in a Latin American city was attempting to locate the position of the placenta in one of his expectant mothers. He injected an air bubble into the baby's amniotic sac and then took x-rays. At one position in which he placed the mother, it so happened that the air bubble covered the baby's face. The whole procedure had no doubt given the little fellow quite a bit of jostling about, and the moment that he had air to inhale and exhale they heard the clear sound of a protesting wail emitting from the uterus. Late that same night, the mother wakened her doctor with a telephone call, to report that when she lay down to sleep the air bubble got over the baby's head again, and he was crying so loud he was keeping both her and her husband awake. The doctor advised her to prop herself upright with pillows so that the air could not reach the baby's head, which was by now in the lower part of the uterus. She spent the remainder of the night dozing upright. The bubble of air slowly dissolved and twenty-three days later the baby was born healthy.

Since you cannot handle him or appeal to him by direct

means, the unborn is quite a tricky little patient. The first few times we attempted to transfuse anemic unborn babies in our hospital, the operating procedure, since it was entirely new and experimental, was somewhat tentative. The surgeon inserted a needle (containing a tiny tube, or catheter, to transmit the blood) through the mother's abdominal wall, into the amniotic sac; then, when he felt the resistance of the baby's abdominal wall, he pressed on through. (The unborn baby can absorb blood directly in his abdomen.) The baby, however, ill though he may have been, felt the needle coming and presented a squirming target. Today the operating technique is designed to catch him by surprise. The surgeon measures precisely on his hand the depth that the needle must go, and then (after checking against an x-ray television screen to make sure his little patient is exactly where he should be) the doctor makes one swift, clean injection which captures the baby before he feels the needle coming toward him. Once he has been pricked, of course, the unborn knows it, and when the doctor removes his hand from the top of the needle after insertion, it wiggles as the baby shows his opinion of the whole proceedings, thus indicating that the needle has found its target The very fine flexible tube, through which the blood cells will be "fed" to the baby's abdomen, is then introduced through the needle. When this is in place the needle is withdrawn. The fine tube may, however, be fitted with a device to keep it in the baby's abdomen several days, so that a long, slow transfusion can be given. Under these circumstances the mother will feel queer little tugs on her skin as her baby moves about at his end of this flexible rope!

The unborn baby, we also discovered, doesn't like the

sensation of cold any better than he likes pain. Since his interior world is snug and warm and maintains a constant temperature, cold is a decidedly uncomfortable change. When a pregnancy requires induced labor, one medical procedure includes the insertion of a catheter via the mother's vagina in order to record the contractions of the uterus and the fetal heartbeat. To cut down chances of infection at this critical stage, the catheter is periodically flushed with an antibiotic solution, which happens to be quite cold. Each time this chilly solution is sent through the catheter, the baby's heartbeat accelerates and he squirms with dismay—just as would a newborn who was plunged into an icy tub.

The baby keeps on moving around and growing within the womb so long as there is nothing to stop him. But in the final weeks of pregnancy, as the baby fills up all the available space, he may be limited both in his movements and in his growth. At seven months if the baby seems very big, you can say that he is a congenitally big baby and probably will grow into a big man or woman. If the mother who is carrying the big baby is small, the baby's growth will be curtailed during the final weeks, and when he is born he will very likely be a big, thin, hungry baby. On the other hand, if his mother's body is adequate he may grow as much as he wants, in which case he will be fleshed out when he is born. It is because of this restriction on growth that the first baby is commonly the smallest, because the tissues offer more resistance to his growth.

As the time for birth nears, most expectant mothers experience a change in the feeling of pregnancy. There is a lessening of the pressure of the fetus, and it no longer seems as though the baby is pushing up against her rib cage. Breathing is easier. This sensation of new comfort is known as "lightening" which may reflect a change in the position of the fetus. Until quite recently it was always assumed that "lightening" was a corollary of another phenomenon called "engagement"—the situation which occurs in late pregnancy when the baby's head actually drops down into the bony pelvis. It seems a natural association that the mother should feel "lighter" when the pressure is removed from her ribs and chest. The most recent medical evidence, however, has established the fact that women often experience this sensation before the baby's head is actually engaged. It has also been proven that when some babies' heads are engaged their mothers feel no difference.

The body has been preparing for birth for quite a long time before what we call labor begins. Throughout pregnancy gentle contractions, which often pass unnoticed by the mother, periodically tighten the womb. As the onset of labor draws near, these contractions come more frequently and vigorously. They are not painful but they may give the mother a sensation of internal tightness, or dragging, which will last from a few seconds to a half a minute.

These contractions produce a twofold effect. They tone up the wall of the womb, preparing it for the hard work of labor. And they line up the baby. This time, his wriggling and protests avail him nothing. He is being slowly but surely stretched out and squeezed by a muscular vise which is far stronger than he. This preparatory work of the womb is entirely autonomic, outside the control of the mother's will. Both she and her baby are being shaped and controlled by an internal function, about which they can do nothing.

Medicine has mastered means to induce this initial onset of labor, and doctors take advantage of it when evidence indicates that the baby's chances will be best if he is born somewhat earlier than term. What doctors have never mastered, however, is control of the reverse problem: how to stop labor once it has started. A certain percentage of women commonly miscarry at twelve to eighteen weeks simply because the cervix relaxes when it should not, and lets the baby pop out. For this sort of premature delivery there is an operation possible in which the doctor merely puts in a stitch to keep the baby where he belongs until he reaches term, and then snips it to allow delivery. But we have as yet found nothing that can reliably control, and stop, the contracting uterus.

It is the aim of obstetrics to keep the unborn in his safe, warm, bacteria-free home as long as he needs it. Although we have marvelous medical means of caring for "preemies" (babies born before term) today, the baby's chances are always much higher if he can be carried to term. Preemies are subject to brain and muscle damage, and respiratory distress—such as the hyaline membrane disease which proved fatal to the Kennedy baby. The babies are not *born* with that disease; they develop it after birth, because they are not properly equipped to cope with their new environment.

We strive to see that our unborn infants arrive at the trauma of birth in the best possible shape, as near to the "normal" seven-and-a-half-pound, twenty-inch newborn as they can possibly be.

By the time the unborn faces birth, he is not nearly so "new" as many people have long imagined. Whatever conditions were present for learning within the womb were taken advantage of, the unborn baby became good at his skills and learned well. If the conditions, or stimuli, were not present, however, the baby did not become proficient, and he will be forced to learn from scratch, with no pre-established body of knowledge into which he can fit the new fact or experience.

At birth, the unborn already knows a great deal about his mouth. He knows about his hands in relation to his mouth, and he can find his face with his hands. He knows perfectly well when he is hurt—although he might not be able to tell precisely where, since localization of sensations does not occur until sometime later, after birth. He knows how to make himself comfortable, and will do his best to achieve comfort, against odds. If things go well for him, he can curl his toes to express his pleasure. If things go badly, he knows how to register protest: by crying and expressing himself with his entire body.

Although fatty tissue is laid down under the baby's skin in the final weeks before birth to cushion his tender parts during birth and keep him warm afterwards, and his head is well designed to mould and accommodate to the pressures of labor and birth, there are many things that upset him: being kept awake, or at least prevented from deep sleep; being pushed and pulled; and, in time being exposed to the chill, strange air outside.

Small wonder that healthy babies greet the new world with loud protest.

chapter six

HOW "NATURAL" WILL CHILDBIRTH BE?

There is considerable confusion, among some medical practitioners as well as the lay public, about the actual process of labor and birth. One of the major misunderstandings has to do with pain. Since pain indicates the presence of contractions it has long been used as a guide to the progress of labor. "The more pain, the better the labor."

This is a legacy from the poorly trained midwives and nurses working with little or no scientific knowledge who, up until the 1920's, handled a large proportion of all obstetrical cases throughout the Western world. In New Zealand, nurses' textbooks at the beginning of the century contained nothing about the anatomy of the female between the waist and the knees. Even though women had already achieved voting rights, it was considered indecent for them to know anything about their own bodies. Nurses managed—or mismanaged—labor according to the criteria of pain, and often induced pain if it was not already present. Even today one will often overhear a modern nurse asking a mother how bad her "pains" are and assuming the labor exists from that alone. Or one may hear the nurse inform the doctor that Mrs. So-and-so is not in labor because the good lady is not apparently suffering discomfort, although placing her hand on the woman's abdomen for five minutes would tell the accurate story.

While pain does indeed depend on the presence of the contraction, the contraction does not depend on the presence of pain. Some women never have pain with pressure on the undilated or partly dilated cervix, while other women find exactly the same degree of pressure agonizing. Between these extremes there is every possible gradation.

The contractions and the accompanying pains are actually two quite distinct issues for the woman who anticipates normal labor. The contractions, which begin days or weeks before the birth stage, are involuntary actions of muscle not ordinarily under the control of the conscious will. Prior to the birth process the muscular uterus begins toning up and strengthening the upper muscles in preparation for the birth; they must be strong enough to overcome the power of the lower muscles, the tight muscular cervix, which has held the baby in throughout pregnancy and must be forced open before he can come out. These early contractions also begin lining up the baby by a gradual and progressive straightening (splinting) of the baby's spine, in preparation for his downward journey. The baby's head, covered by membranes and protected by the forewaters, is pushed down into the ring of bone called the pelvic brim, which is the first obstacle that he must pass, and impinges against the muscular cervix, the second obstacle. When the birth process actually starts, the contractions continue to work in exactly the same way, except that they take on a regular pattern which gradually gains momentum. As the uterine contents (the baby's head and the forewaters) are driven against the closed cervix, the internal pressure causes pain.

This labor pain is known as deep—as opposed to bright—pain. Deep pain is not easily localized, and has a dull, agonizing quality. While bright pain makes one act quickly, due to the quick release of adrenaline, deep pain makes the individual want to curl up, and perhaps groan a little.

Labor pains are of great medical value, acting as a signal that birth is near. It is a warning for the primitive woman to come in from the fields, or for the woman from our culture to pack her bag for the hospital. We can only assume that in the most widely known of all stories of birth, Mary's labor pain did not commence until after she had set out on her journey to Jerusalem. The rare woman who experiences no pain at all is likely to end up bearing her baby unattended in the back of a taxicab or in a public toilet.

Birth itself, referred to by the obstetric fraternity as the second stage of labor, is in some ways quite distinct from the first stage, and yet it is a continuation of the same process. Again we have to distinguish between pain and contractions. The pain in the first stage of labor is caused by pressure on the undilated (or partially dilated) cervix. Since the second stage commences with the full dilation of the cervix, it follows that the pain from the dilating cervix is no longer present. The woman feels a change in sensation, a little pause. In the birth phase the uterine contractions go on as in the first stage, although the spacing may change and the uterus itself will retract in width with each contraction. There is a tremendous variation in the pain experienced during birth. From the woman with a well-molded, smallish baby and good relaxation of the pelvic floor and a well-softened introitus, who enjoys delivery, to the woman with a long labor, poor contractions, a baby "coming the wrong way," or a low pain threshold, there is all the difference in the world. The second stage may not be painful—or it may test the unaided woman to the limits of her endurance. There is no physical and little physiological relationship between the pain of the first stage (labor) and that of the second (birth).

Since pain has classically been associated with childbirth, women eagerly accepted the promise of a pain-free birth, through the use of full anesthesia, when it was first introduced. In our mothers' day, it was routine for the attending obstetrician to administer full anesthesia, and assist all deliveries. Doctors considered themselves failures if their patients felt—or could remember—the birth. Women woke up the next day and were handed a neatly bundled baby, like a package at the supermarket, and had no memory of delivering him.

This lack of involvement in the birth troubled women, however, and in reaction to such complete medical management, an alternate to anesthesia was introduced by Dr. G. D. Read in England. With Dr. Read's method women were "educated for childbirth" and encouraged to participate throughout without the anesthesia. Read's theory was that childbirth pain was largely a product of fear, and that if women could be trained to overcome their fear by a series of pre-natal exercises, which he felt had physiological value, they would be able to go through labor and birth without pain. He also claimed that the birth process would be less subject to complications. As

it turned out, Dr. Read had to resort to operative interference (forceps) with his cases just as often as any other
obstetrician, and in many cases his patients required pain
relief. But he did make a large contribution to obstetrics
by proving to the medical world that women do not invariably seek the head-in-the-sand approach to childbirth.
Emphasizing the sense of joy and achievement in birth,
rather than the traditional fear, Read helped put childbearing back into its proper, and in that sense "natural,"
perspective.

Many women have faithfully followed the course of
instruction provided by the "natural childbirth" school
and felt they benefited from it. Others have experienced
only frustration and a disappointing sense of failure at
the time of birth. They were probably both correct, depending on how their individual labors went.

The basic fallacy of the "natural childbirth" theory lies
in the fact that no two labors proceed identically, and
it is therefore both impossible and unwise to attempt to
anticipate precisely what will happen. The worst effect
of the training is the sense of failure it has produced in
women who prepared for a painless "natural" birth only
to find they required forceps and pain-relieving drugs to
bear their babies. If a woman has preconceived ideas of
childbirth and has ambitions for her own role in it, and it
does not proceed as she anticipated, she is apt to experience a sense of inadequacy and disappointment.

No matter how zealously women train for childbirth,
fifteen percent of all women who go into labor are destined to encounter mechanical or physiological complications that are quite beyond their control. No amount of
training will alter the fact that a certain number of births
will require major obstetrical interference, from an order

for a Caesarian section on down to the use of forceps. Women should not feel disgraced or let down if forceps are necessary. It seems foolish to hear a mother complain that she had to undergo a forceps delivery when indeed there would have been much more to complain about had there been no forceps there when they were needed. Obstetric forceps are not mighty tweezers used to contort and extract, but fine metal blades which fit in neatly where there is no room for an accoucheur's hand.

Dr. Read actually had considerable success with his patients, but not for the reason that he originally supposed. Read's great success was due to the fact that he made his patients feel happy and confident; he kept them physically fit through exercises; but most important of all, his patients were never left alone in labor.

At the bedsides of birth and of death kindly company is the best of all commodities. Ideally, it is the husband's role, as partner in parenthood, to provide his wife with the comfort and strength of his presence. This, of course, depends on the husband. If he is not suited for this role, a kindly nurse or therapist can provide the reassurance that the mother needs. But plans should be made in advance so that the mother will never be left alone during labor or delivery.

Since Read's theory was first introduced, group classes for mothers have sprung up all over the Western world (ninety percent of all pregnant women in Russia attend them) that range in their childbirth training from simply physical therapy to self-hypnosis, designed to counteract birth fear. In hypno-therapy, women are trained to produce a state of self-delusion or self-hypnosis to blot out pain. This is based on the idea that since all pain is felt at the level of the brain, and the brain can only receive a certain number of impulses at one time, a woman can be taught to bombard her brain with so many impulses, including thoughts, of her own making, that pain sensations cannot reach a level in her conscious mind. It is the same type of phenomenon that we encounter with an overloaded telephone exchange.

Another, more recent development is the Le Maze school of psycho-prophylaxis. In this method a great deal more emphasis is given to breathing techniques and less to learning relaxation. In effect, relaxation is achieved through breathing. As so often happens in medicine, an effective method of therapy was developed before the physiology was fully worked out. The treatment was arrived at by trial and error and not from a knowledge of how the uterus altered shape in labor. It is now known that during contractions the top of the uterus remains at the same height but pushes forward against the abdominal wall from the inside. If this wall is held tightly, the uterus is prevented from swinging forward to its fullest extent, which has the same effect as pressing down on the top, a maneuver known from antiquity to increase cervical pain. If, on the other hand, the abdominal wall is relaxed, the uterus swings fully and the pain is lessened. In learning to concentrate on breathing, mothers are taught to modify the pressure according to the extent of uterine activity, and effective pain relief is achieved both by avoiding pressure on top of the contracting uterus, and by avoiding awareness of pain. The decompression suit, used in South Africa, relieves pain by removal of pressure only, since it lifts the abdominal wall off the contracting uterus. The fact that this suit is often all that is needed is further evidence of the individuality of pain.

Each specialist involved in obstetrical cases has his

own, somewhat one-sided view of what is most important. When an obstetrician designs an ante-natal course of instruction, he frequently takes the labor and birth out of perspective in its relation to overall motherhood and dwells on this brief period to the exclusion of other factors. Certainly he will stress the hygiene of pregnancy; he may recommend mothercraft classes, and he is sometimes vaguely aware of the presence of the father in the background. But always uppermost in his mind are the final stages of labor and the birth of the baby, which, from his point of view, are the essential climax to the whole affair.

While it is helpful to understand the general course of labor so that it won't seem surprising or strange, detailed descriptions are quite pointless, since there is no way to anticipate how a particular labor will go. Such teaching can even be dangerous to one's peace of mind since variations of preconceived ideas are apt to be frightening. So far as the first stage of labor is concerned, the long process of opening up the cervix in preparation for the descent and expulsion of the baby, it is only necessary to understand that it lasts a considerable time before the birth stage will be reached. There is little training that one can provide for this stage of labor, beyond education in ways to relax and breathe during contractions, and an understanding that will equip the mother with an attitude of calm acceptance. The best way to pass the early waiting period is to be active with small chores around the house until the pains are coming at ten-minute intervals and it is time to check into the hospital.

A physiotherapist's view of good maternal education entails plenty of exercises for pregnancy, labor and birth, and also for the post-natal stage. This is very useful, provided that it does not, like the natural childbirth school, produce an introspective mother who dwells so much on herself that she forgets the purpose of pregnancy: the baby. The therapist's zeal about the benefits of exercise should not lead women to believe that exercise in itself will have any effect on the physical course of their labor, other than to prevent post-natal stiffness of the hips and thighs.

It is not normal for labor to be a feat of strength for voluntarily controlled muscles, even during the birth stage. Birth actually involves a very delicate coordination between the contractions of the uterus and the relaxation of the pelvic floor. The more perfect this coordination is, the less conscious effort is required.

The idea that women could contribute to their deliveries through concerted "pushing" was based on the belief that the uterus descends during the birth, and that pressure on the top (an attendant pushing on the fundus and straining efforts by the mother) would help expel the baby. Thanks to a series of x-rays by Dr. Narik in Vienna, it has been conclusively established that the uterus does not descend during birth, and the cervix, which was formerly thought to remain in place, does come down with the baby's head. But pushing by an attendant during the delivery, or straining by the mother before the final stage of birth is reached, only increase the mother's pain and cut off the baby's blood and oxygen supply.

The "pushing" theory was also a result in part of observation of four-legged animals grunting and straining to give birth, which was assumed to be "natural" for women as well. The animal's physiological structure is, however, quite different. It carries its young in a non-muscular uterus that rests on the abdominal wall and is slung like a hammock from four legs. Since there is no chance of the fetus falling out of this hammock, there is no need for a tight muscular ring, like the human cervix, to hold the baby in.

Human beings, standing on two legs, have had to make important adjustments to a more complicated childbirth. There is a complete ring of bone (the pelvic brim) to support the two legs in the upright position, and a ring of muscle (the cervix) to hold in the fetus—both of which the baby must navigate during birth.

The animal mother presents no such barriers to the birth of her young. She does, however, have to move the offspring from the abdominal position, through the birth canal and the lower vaginal opening. Since her uterus is not muscular, the whole process of expulsion depends on bearing-down efforts of the mother, using her abdominal muscles and her diaphragm. She expels her baby from her body by pushing, straining, and grunting.

The human mother, however, accomplishes nothing by such early straining efforts until the cervix is fully dilated. It is only at the end of the delivery, as the baby's head is actually emerging from her body through the introitus (the vaginal entrance), that the mother can exert conscious control. Then, if the mechanical conditions are right—which include both the size of the baby in proportion to her body, and the position of the baby— she can contribute to the delivery. Even then, no more pushing is usually necessary than that which the body does irresistibly, as in defecation. If she has had babies before, she may be able to deliver voluntarily and find the experience pleasurable—and even erotic. With the trend toward smaller families and population control, it is unlikely that many women in the future will remember birth as erotically pleasurable.

The aim of pre-natal exercise classes should not be to ease labor—since many investigators more scientific than Dr. Read have now proved that no reduction of labor difficulties can be attributed to exercise—but simply to maintain muscle tone. Giving birth, like playing a first game of tennis, is very apt to make muscles stiff, unless one has "warmed up" a bit in advance. A regular routine of exercise carried out throughout pregnancy and following the birth can insure that childbearing and childbirth will do no permanent harm to the body. Exercise carried out properly not only creates muscles that are healthy and strong enough to achieve sustained contractions during birth; exercise can also set a goal of lasting importance: permanent muscle tone.

Today most maternity hospitals do provide ante-natal classes run by trained physiotherapists. Strenuous "keep fit" type exercises are not recommended. But a few simple ones, performed slowly and rhythmically, such as crook-lying and the pelvic tilt, are very good. They prevent muscular stiffness following birth, and help return the body as quickly as possible to pre-pregnancy state after the baby is delivered. Other exercises are aimed at reducing the possibility of varicose veins, and at making postural adjustments to the body weight.

Good posture can be practiced at all times to prevent the horrid hollow in the back that some women acquire during pregnancy, which looks dreadful and causes uncomfortable backache. It also helps to develop the habit of picking things up correctly, by maintaining a straight back and lowering the body weight at the knees, so that the weight is borne by the large thigh muscles and the stress on the back is relieved.

There is no excuse today for the gross misshapen bodies that were once attributed to childbearing. Many women, especially city dwellers, have appalling body shapes from their early twenties on. A considerable amount of the gynecological disability suffered by Western women from middle age onward is directly due to poor muscle tone, sagging, obese abdomens, and the constant use of corsets and girdles which press internal organs into wrong places. Ideally, awareness of the importance of physical fitness, and exercise to maintain muscle tone which is practiced in pregnancy should become a habitual part of a woman's daily life. During my third pregnancy I recall a very beautiful and happy-looking young woman who was doing exercises with our hospital physiotherapist at a class I attended as a trained observer. She told me that this was her eighth pregnancy and that she had attended exercise classes on the seven previous occasions, and kept up a modified program of exercise between times. From hers and many subsequent cases, I am convinced that a good strong body (and perhaps some stretch marks on the abdominal skin in one woman out of four) should be the only physical signs of motherhood as opposed to spinsterhood. We have a lot yet to learn from the East, where the women stay neat and trim in their middle years and never suffer from prolapses of the uterus.

A good diet and weight watching should also become a habit carried over from pregnancy. Exercise must be accompanied by diet to be effective, but one rarely sees an obese man or woman who has come to enjoy physical activity.

There are probably as many different experiences in

childbirth as there are pregnant women. Most doctors agree that when a woman is to be conscious for even a part of her labor, she should be taught breathing and relaxation techniques. The amount of pain relief (given in the form of drugs) will vary from doctor to doctor, and from hospital to hospital. Ideally, it should suit the individual case, since thresholds to pain differ enormously. Great advances in pharmacology of recent years have produced drugs that will relieve the pain of labor without producing unconsciousness. The mother's endurance will also depend on the length of the labor, the time between the contractions, and her general tolerance. When labor is long and tedious, a sedative to induce sleep at least during the night may be given in addition to regular administrations of pain-relieving drugs. This is necessary to help the baby sleep, too, for regular contractions will undoubtedly keep him from the periods of deep sleep to which he is accustomed.

Due to a misunderstanding of the childbirth process, women are still sometimes given full anesthesia for delivery. Pain relief is required in the first stage of labor, not the second. Self-administered nitrous oxide and oxygen may be used for the second stage where necessary to help the mother relax, but the blotting out of consciousness is very rarely indicated.

The most satisfactory labors are often seen with women having their second or third child, when, after two or three hours of good, strong, regular contractions, the cervix dilates fully and the second stage is reached. Labors of this sort are well within the bearable range for both mother and baby. The mother is not left alone because it is during this time that her husband gets her to the hospital, the staff prepares her for delivery, the doctor arrives, and all is made ready. Though the pain may be severe, there is so much distraction that the mother's mind is not left free to concentrate on it.

A first labor is always an unknown. It is rarely quick and efficient. Good ante-natal care can very much reduce the risk of an abnormal labor, but with the variability in the baby's size and position, and the force of the uterine contractions, it is difficult to promise a normal labor and birth. We obviously cannot leave an abnormal birth process to take its "natural" course. It would be disastrous. Women having a first baby are better off not to set their hearts too much on a "natural" birth, since the length of labor may prove too exhausting if they do not use some pain-relieving drugs. It would be foolish, indeed, for the mother to exhaust herself so much in labor that she could not enjoy seeing and fondling the new baby.

If possible, prospective parents should become acquainted with the hospital where the baby is to be born before the expectant mother actually checks in for the birth. Large maternity hospitals entail so much administration these days—with appointment clerks, record clerks, supply clerks, kitchen staff, cleaning staff, household managers, and canteen workers—that there would be enough to occupy this lay staff if no patients came near the hospital for weeks. And this list does not include the complex nursing hierarchy. For the person viewing this gigantic operation for the first time, it might seem that the patients themselves could be little more than soulless machines to be serviced. Yet, a tour around the hospital helps them see that, despite its awesome appearance, the hospital is a friendly place. To help the mother withstand the inevitable stress of giving birth in a hospital, we also like to show our new parents films of actual births that have taken place there. This familiarizes them with the delivery room and the medical procedures, so that it won't all seem so strange and terrifying when they are wheeled in. In this way the film serves the same purpose as putting airline pilots through "mock-up crashes." If the mother knows what the place looks like and how procedures are carried out, she will be less tense when her time arrives. The pictures also serve another purpose. By showing what trauma birth will be for the baby, they take the mother's mind off herself.

Before she enters a hospital the modern young woman should have learned about the variations that birth may bring, and she should not expect that her body will invariably be able to deal with the mechanical problems that might arise. She should be both confident and willing to accept pain-relieving drugs and manipulative help, if her medical attendant prescribes them. Since we have long ago given up nature's standards for disease, death, and survival, we prescribe what seems on good evidence to reduce maternal and fetal suffering the most.

There are many ways in which the baby's father can help the expectant mother throughout her pregnancy. He can see that she is getting sufficient exercise, that she is not putting on too much weight, that she is drinking enough fluids each day. With his more detached view of the pregnancy, he can also help his wife maintain an overall interest in it, without letting her go overboard on one phase or another. Some women have a tendency to become "specialists" in anything they do. When pregnant, they "specialize" in breast feeding or in "natural" childbirth education or in labor pains, to the detriment of a total interest in their baby. The husband will be doing both his wife and his child a service if he reminds her that long after these specializations are over, the demanding role of motherhood will still carry on.

In their concentration on the day of delivery, many obstetricians and ante-natal instructors take the role of motherhood considerably out of context. Birth, while a wonderful accomplishment in which a woman can take justifiable pride, should not be dwelt upon to the exclusion of the total pregnancy. With today's medical techniques which insure such a high rate of survival and care, most any woman can survive her labor whether she wants the baby or not, whether she is frightened or joyful, whether she is a reluctant, unwed mother or a motherly matron.

For the first months of her pregnancy, it is quite natural that the mother—especially if this is her first baby —will think about herself. So many things that she can feel and see are happening to her own body. But as birth approaches, she should be thinking about what she will do with her baby after she has given birth. The goal of raising a healthy child should be the expectant mother's concern, rather than the "day of delivery."

chapter seven

THE STORM

Part I: Mother and Doctor

Many expectant mothers are disappointed because their obstetricians fail to provide them with a blow-by-blow battle plan for the birth. If the doctor sounds vague about the delivery it is not because he lacks knowledge. The doctor actually has a very wide range of things that he can do. But he does not know what will be required until he sees what is happening, and how the delivery progresses. From his standpoint, the birth is rather like a football game; the coach and the team have a strategy mapped out, but their actual tactics on the playing field may depend upon what the opposition presents. In some cases, for example, the doctor has information beforehand which dictates that the baby should best be delivered by a pre-planned Caesarian section (surgically, through the abdomen of the mother). There are other occasions, however, when a Caesarian only becomes necessary after the birth process has already begun. I recall one such instance where there was no previous indication that such a measure would be necessary. The mother, who had been a professional acrobat before her marriage, was in superior physical shape. The fetus had developed without any complication, to term. But when the mother entered the second stage of labor, the doctor suddenly discovered that her muscles inside her abdominal cavity—the psoas muscles—were so highly overdeveloped that it was impossible for the baby's head to pass them naturally. A Caesarian was necessary to deliver a live baby.

Both Caesarian section (probably named after the Latin *caesim*, meaning "by cutting," and not related to Julius) and the use of forceps in delivery dealt originally with death rather than life. Caesarians were invented in order to get the dead baby out of the dead mother for separate burials to satisfy religious precepts. Today, a Caesarian is a fairly common and relatively safe medical procedure which is used to deliver babies who might encounter severe trouble being born normally. A number of women have had as many as six or more babies in this fashion. Similarly, forceps were first designed as a means of delivering dead babies. Now they are habitually used to assist the baby over any undue obstacles. Most good obstetricians, however, would always prefer that the baby could manage to get himself delivered without such surgical assistance.

Just as pregnancy itself is dictated by the fetus, so to a great extent is birth. We have as yet found nothing in the mother's body which triggers the onset of labor. The doctor does not arbitrarily deliver a baby. The mother and the baby together bring the baby forth. Ideally, the obstetrician's role is to stand by. He is there—like an insurance policy—in case anything goes wrong.

The first stage of labor is officially designated when the mother's uterine contractions begin to dilate the cervix. Since the woman has no arbitrary control over the onset or the progress of her labor, no one can state definitely when the first stage will begin. The total gestation period is best estimated in *weeks* from the last normal menstrual period. Pregnancy then normally lasts anywhere from 37 to 43 weeks, with an average duration of 40 weeks. A great deal of confusion arises if months are used, as these may be calendar or lunar and important fractions are discarded.

When labor does start, the contractions are recognizably different from those the mother has previously experienced. They take on a rhythmic quality. While continuing to harden the womb and align the baby for birth, they now at regular intervals press the uterine contents against the tightly closed neck of the womb, the cervix, opening it little by little in preparation for the baby's head —the largest part of the fetus—to pass through. The rhythm may seem quite slow at first, with the contractions coming only at fifteen-minute intervals and lasting about thirty seconds. But in time the interval between them shortens and they last longer—forty or more seconds—and grow stronger.

Sometimes labor starts at night and it takes a while for the contractions to rouse the mother from sleep. Mothers occasionally become aware that labor has begun not because of contractions, but because they pass a pinkish mucous ("show") which indicates that the womb has already opened a little. At other times, the bag of waters breaks at the very onset of labor and the mother knows that her time is near when she feels the sudden gush of water. Once labor has been established most women experience severe periodic pain which lasts about one-half minute out of every five or ten minutes. Relief can be obtained by complete relaxation during the contractions, accompanied by upper abdominal breathing. When the contractions are spaced ten minutes apart, it is time to call the doctor or hospital.

With the first baby, labor can be expected to last between nine and eighteen hours. The first few of these hours may be spent at home, working at odd jobs around the house, which can be managed quite well when there are only six contractions per hour. During the contractions, however, the mother should sit down and relax completely. While it is hard to relax when contractions are frequent and painful, it is very important to make every effort to do so, since nothing can be gained by trying to push or walk or jump to speed up the process. In fact, it might well cause damage to push before the cervix has been properly dilated, and certainly causes congestion or swelling of blood vessels in the pelvis.

For the obstetrician, who wishes to bring both his patients through in top form, the mother's labor pain is essential, since it provides fair warning that the birth is imminent and it enables her to contact her doctor and to get to the hospital. Or, if she has already checked in, it gives her plenty of time to alert her attendants that she is ready for the delivery suite.

The doctor also hopes that the second stage of labor will not proceed too swiftly. The type of delivery that worries him most is the rapid, precipitous birth wherein the baby is expelled explosively from his warm, wet, weightless world into the pressures of air and gravity, and his body does not have sufficient time to make a proper adjustment. The great danger in this sort of delivery is that the too-swift expulsion may cause undue pressure change within the baby's brain. A longer, slower descent gives the baby a far better chance at health.

The doctor has two patients during the birth, the baby and the mother. Hopefully, what is good for one will also be good for the other. But this is not always true. A swift delivery might be easy on the mother but dangerous for her child. And a Caesarian section, which is quite easy on the baby, multiplies the risk for his mother. While this operation is still safer than an appendectomy, most obstetricians will strive for a delivery through the birth canal if at all possible.

The obstetrician's rules for delivery are governed by the "Three P's": the Powers, which are the mother's contractions; the Passenger, which is the baby; and the Passages, which include the whole of the soft tissue and bony limits of the birth canal. The emergencies he watches for include cord complications, fetal distress and failure to make steady progress. Certain positions of the baby, for instance breech presentations, may require that the doctor intervene. He has much that he can do appropriate to any situation. Sometimes a combination of minor factors may justify intervention. The doctor decides whether or not to take over and assist with the delivery by reckoning the amount of risk involved with mother or child. If it appears that there may be a risk in leaving things alone, the doctor will intervene. It is essentially preventive medicine.

The quality of the contractions—which is purely a physiological phenomenon over which no one, mother, baby, or doctor, has any control—is very important. If the contractions are good, other problems such as an unusually small pelvis, or an extra-large baby, or a baby who is lying in an unfavorable position, can be overcome without surgical assistance. If the contractions work well toward the birth, the mother is able to stretch and the baby can mold. The baby is quite plastic at this stage and given sufficient momentum from the contractions, he can adjust astonishingly well to the business of entering the outside world by whatever restricting labyrinth he encounters.

Until the cervix is fully dilated, all force comes from these involuntary uterine contractions. Most of labor and delivery is autonomic and unconscious, for the body functions outside the control of the conscious mind. Many women have been successfully delivered of their babies when they were unconscious from brain or spinal injury. Like digestion, breathing, the beating of the heart, birth is, to a great extent, an involuntary function.

It is only in the second stage of labor, during the birth of the baby, that the contractions can be aided by the mother's voluntary "pushing down" efforts. But this is still predominately a reflex action which is triggered by the pressure of the baby's head against the pelvic floor, and by the tendency to empty the body. Hormonal secretions from the placenta have made the tissues capable of stretching. Whether or not the mother does assist voluntarily at this stage, her body will continue nonetheless to work to expel the baby. Women can go through labor heavily sedated, unconscious, or in a coma.

Good preparation for childbirth should include color slides of, or visits with, newly born babies, rather than practice for the delivery. The sort of exercises where pregnant women lie propped up on pillows holding their legs akimbo, pushing down forcefully to a count of seven to ten, are very unphysiological—and the psychology, too, seems to have gone astray. Lying on the back in this fashion with the uterus fully occupied (instead of half empty as it is during actual delivery) causes considerable obstruction to the return flow of blood in the great veins (inferior vena cava). Pushing down in itself increases the blood in the pelvic area, so that the combination of more blood and less return flow will severely tax the veins, and heighten the chances of developing piles in the rectum or vulval varicosities. There is also the added chance of weakening the attachments of the pelvic viscera and setting the stage for a prolapse (dropping down) of the internal organs in later life. The unborn baby may also be adversely affected by the lowered oxygen saturation which can be observed in the mother's blood stream during breathholding and pushing efforts.

More and more doctors are coming to believe that the pushing effort in delivery should be a reflex act, not trained behavior. The mother should know what to expect, but, more important, she should be ready to receive her newborn baby joyfully.

The birth itself, for the mother, is relatively free from internal pain. It is also relatively short, lasting from ten minutes to one and a half hours. The mother can recognize the change from the first to the second stage of labor when she experiences the almost uncontrollable urge to push downward. Fortunately, when she does reach the birth stage she can push, and thus help the doctor and her baby. There is, for many women, a moment of triumph and exhilaration when they feel the baby finally released from their body.

For those who attend the birth, the safe arrival of a new baby brings an inevitable thrill. Certain doctors and nurses would not specialize in obstetrics unless they had come to be so moved by birth. Having themselves long ago replaced any feelings of squeamishness with appreciative awe, the medical team may be somewhat nonplussed at a mother's first reaction to the sight of her newborn baby.

It is a help to the new mother if she has seen other very small babies. When she first sees her own baby, he will be wet, streaked with mucuous and perhaps blood from

LABOR—THE FIRST STAGE

This is the sequence in labor. When the uterus contracts the baby is splinted out and the presenting part (head) is applied to the cervix. The cervix is the first barrier. Opening the first barrier is called **the first stage.**

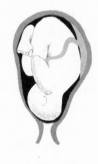

1
The relaxed uterus baby is like a "rag doll."

2
Contraction. Baby becomes a "tin soldier."

3
Relaxed again.

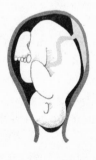

4
Contraction. The cervix is gradually opened.

5
Relaxed again.

6
Contraction near the end of first stage.

BIRTH—THE SECOND STAGE

As the fetal head has now passed through the pelvic brim and is resting on the pelvic floor, we are looking at the back of the baby's head instead of the side, as before. The head must turn through 30 degrees during the descent from the pelvic brim to the pelvic floor.

The uterus does not shorten but becomes narrower as the contents descend. The lower opening (cervix) of the uterus descends with the baby's head.

7
Interval. The uterine walls present a wavy outline.

8
Contraction. The uterine walls are straighter and so is the fetal spine.

9
The baby does not descend the length of the vagina during this phase, as was previously taught. Having reached the introitus at the end of the first stage, he is now pushed through this second barrier.

the already separated placenta. His body will be caked with whitish vernix, the barrier cream that protects his skin in the watery environment of the uterus; this is washed away when he is bathed. He may be quite blue until he has cried a bit. But he is alive. That is the thrill. For the mother, the relief that labor is over and the baby is alive and well is momentous. This is the moment to crown all moments.

The baby's father should be brought in as soon as possible to share the general joy of birth. Some husbands attend the birth, seated at the head end of the couch, but this procedure is not available at all hospitals.

Once the baby's body has been delivered, the only thing left in the mother's uterus is the placenta, which is about the size of a dinner plate but malleable. While the uterus was expelling the baby, it was also simultaneously contracting and retracting, already in the process of shortening to its pre-pregnant dimensions. As the uterus shrinks in size, the area where the placenta was attached also shrinks, and the placenta usually shears off from the wall of the uterus as the baby's body is delivered. If the placenta should adhere to the interior wall after the baby is delivered, the doctor may have to fetch it out. Because it usually shears off from the wall before the baby is fully delivered there is some bleeding, which may make the baby look rather messy when first seen.

Since there is still an interchange of blood between the placenta and the baby via the umbilical cord, the cord is clamped off quickly to prevent the baby from losing any blood back to the placenta. At one time it was medical practice to wait for a moment, on the assumption that the baby would receive a final surge of blood from the placenta. But it was found that the reverse might just as well happen, and the baby would lose some of his much-needed blood.

When the placenta has been expelled from the uterus, the final stage of labor is finished. The mother, who has usually had a chance to hold her baby, is through with her job for the moment, and she now needs a sponge bath, a change into a fresh nightgown, and a visit with her husband. After that she needs a good, long rest. The baby does not need the mother right now, for he, too, must rest.

Following the delivery of her baby, the mother might expect to feel elated. She has just shed maybe twelve or so pounds or more of weight, for one thing. She has successfully given birth to a live child. It should be a very great moment for her, but psychologically this is not always so. The mother may, whether she likes it or not, feel washed-out, dizzy, feverish, or just plain drugged.

Following the birth great changes must occur in the mother's body as it restores to the non-pregnant state. For both mother and baby there is a change from a wet, warm internal environment to one that is a little cooler and progressively drier. Large volumes of urine accumulate in the mother's bladder after delivery, and this organ may become quite dangerously distended if not regularly emptied. There is a heavy blood-stained discharge from the placental site; this is maximal during the first day or two and eases off gradually after the first week. Regular contractions, quite often painful, carry this discharge away. These contractions are called "after pains," and they represent exactly the same contractions that the uterus undergoes during both menstruation and childbirth. The pain has the same cause: it is produced when the uterus attempts to force a bulky mass through a closed, or partly closed, cervix. The internal hormone pitocin causes contractions, and it is poured out from the pituitary gland when the mother nurses her baby. At these times, a recently delivered woman may momentarily double up with a crampy after pain.

Shivering attacks may occur in the day or so following childbirth, as may sweating, when the mother wakes with her nightgown soaked. Both conditions indicate that the body temperature is seesawing back and forth as the thermostat is set for a smaller furnace. The loss of stored fluid comes about both because placentally produced hormones have been removed and because the mother's body has less need to dissipate heat. The less constant aftereffect of childbirth is soreness of the introitus (the external entrance of the vagina), which becomes progressively less with succeeding children.

Since such great readjustments occur within the mother's body following delivery, a full twenty-four-hour period of complete rest and full nursing care is indicated. This period may be extended whenever delivery has been difficult or a Caesarian section has been required. However, bruised tissues recover much more quickly if exercised—as anyone who has sprained an ankle at any time will recall—and graduated exercises, short walks such as trips to the toilet and shower, are indicated after the first day or so. Very often much of the discomfort following delivery is due to the stiffness in the hips as a result of prolonged periods of lying in the unnatural position required when a woman is delivered under anaesthetic. In this case her legs are held akimbo by leg-holders, and although she is insensible to hip trauma at the time, she will almost certainly feel the effects afterward. Doctors who advise their patients to undergo an anesthetized delivery should also advise preparatory exercises such as pelvic rocking and squatting during the ante-natal pe-period. Just as in the case of Caesarian section, an anaes-thetized delivery may seem easier to an uninitiated or ig-norant woman, but she will pay for it afterward with discomfort. It also seems a pity to exchange the exhilara-tion of a stupendous event for the undignified, helpless coma of anaesthesia during delivery just because one is too lazy to attend ante-natal instruction—or too afraid of life.

The mother should begin a program of regular post-natal exercises a day or so after her baby is born, in order to get the stretched muscles back into trim, and to pre-vent possible post-natal complications, such as "milk leg" (an infection of the veins caused by inertia) or inconti-nence of urine. The exercises that are important at this time are relatively the same ones that she followed dur-ing pregnancy: those designed to strengthen the abdom-inal and pelvic muscles and to maintain good posture. Deep breathing and leg exercises are also essential to pre-vent circulatory complications while the mother is still in the hospital. It also helps if the mother spends at least a few minutes each day lying on her face, with a pillow tucked under her stomach.

The uterus is at the level of the navel after the birth, and it gradually subsides. The discharge from the womb, which lasts four to six weeks, is helped along by contrac-tions of the womb until it entirely disappears. The ova-rian rhythm—ovulation, then menstruation—will recom-mence at some time from six weeks to six months following childbirth.

The mother's body returns gradually to the non-preg-nant state. The breasts need comfortable support and should not be permitted to sag except during feedings. The milk will come in on the third day after the birth, and the supply of milk can be improved by feeding the baby when he is hungry and by seeing him regularly.

Mothers cannot afford to spend months "getting over" the baby. Their husbands need them. Their other children, if they have them, need them. And for the mother's own physical and mental health she should get back into top form as quickly as possible.

Tiredness is the most common single symptom following childbirth, and it affects both mother and baby. There are two types of tiredness: one, the natural weariness following the hard physical labor of childbirth, which, combined with broken sleep while the baby is young, is apt to produce exhaustion, or simply a feeling of being "always tired." There is every reason why both the mother and baby should experience fatigue tiredness: the baby, because his efforts to obtain food and to work against gravity are so exhausting; the mother, because her day is longer and her normal sleep pattern is interrupted. This fatigue, however, is entirely reversible for the mother. Either she simply puts up with it until the baby sleeps for longer periods at night, or, with a considerate husband's assistance, she can take a night off once in a while and have a twelve-hour sleep.

The second form of tiredness, which is more akin to apathy or depression, is much more serious. This is the sort of dragging, listless feeling that stems, not from loss of sleep, but from a feeling of incompetence, inadequacy, and a general inability to cope with the situation: the baby. If this is a first baby, the mother's life has indeed changed inexorably. Time she once had for herself is no longer hers. She may suffer a sense of guilt because of her ambivalent feelings toward her baby: she loves him, but he is still a stranger to her and she begrudges the time taken from her own interests and comfort.

The subject of this type of tiredness has difficulty pursuing one job or one line of thought to its conclusion. She is too anxious to get to something else to finish what is at hand. At night she does not rest fully. Fears and anxieties abound, and during the normal periods of lighter sleep, they rouse her to full consciousness, so that she rises in the morning feeling as though she has not slept at all. The light of laughter fades from her life and she becomes irritable. The course of this syndrome is downhill unless it is arrested. If a husband finds his wife "always tired" he should try and assess whether this is indeed fatigue, or the more serious state of anxiety. If the latter, the mother must be persuaded to set her sights a little lower.

For her baby needs her concentrated affection and attention now. He needs her more now, in fact, in the days and weeks immediately following his birth, than he will need her again in his entire life.

chapter eight

THE STORM

Part II: Birth for the Baby

The first stage of labor probably means a good deal of interrupted sleep for the baby. While his mother may experience pain as the cervix dilates, the process merely makes the baby uncomfortable. He has by now become accustomed to periodic contractions of the womb, which have been occurring for some time. When the constraint of these contractions wears off, the baby may wiggle in response. This is why some women confuse fetal movement with early contractions, because they seem to come together, while other women are quite well aware of the distinction. It is through those occasional pre-labor contractions that the uterus succeeds in corralling the baby into a longitudinal lie, which will be best for birth.

As the womb prepares for the birth, the baby's position becomes progressively more restricted. The uterus elongates and thins, as does the rolled-up baby who is straightened during contractions, and the baby's head is forced down against the cervix. This straightening of the spine, called "splinting," is not unlike the action of a watchspring imbedded in a tennis ball. If you were to press each side of the ball, the spring would straighten out as the ball changed from round to long and thin.

Now, for the first time, the baby is no longer benignly protected by his surrounding sac of fluid. For, as the cervix dilates, his head is pushed against it, and beyond this opening lie the unfamiliar pressures of gravity and air. Once the baby's membrane ruptures and the fluid is lost, he is much more constrained than before. Until then he had a steadily diminishing choice of position, but now the uterus dominates him. He has no freedom of action, no familiar fluid to bathe him, and he is slowly but surely being squeezed against unfamiliar bony areas of his mother's body. As the contracting waves beat upon him he has no choice but to be forced forward.

Fortunately the baby is better equipped at this time than he will ever again be to withstand physical duress. It may well be the worst beating he will get in his entire life.

It was once thought that during birth the baby was physiologically inert, and that he simply popped out, under hydraulic pressure, as a cork does from a champagne bottle or toothpaste from a tube. We now know that this is not true. The baby has before him a harrowing voyage that contains three major obstacles which he must navigate: the cervix, the bony pelvis, and finally the perineum (the tissue surrounding the vagina), each of which subjects him to pressure. He encounters the cervix throughout his mother's first stage of labor, when the periodic contractions of the uterus and the consequent straightening of his spine force his head tightly against the opening cervix. The second obstacle is the curving canal of his mother's bony pelvis. It is quite common that at the onset of labor the baby's head is already down in the pelvis and his head is said to be engaged or fixed (a position that is more easily determined before labor by examining the woman standing). If this is true, the baby starts labor with a part of the birth already negotiated. The curved axis of the canal and the form of the walls force the baby to rotate in order to negotiate the canal. That is, the baby's head normally enters the top of the canal facing to one side but emerges at the bottom facing backward—or, less commonly, forward. Moreover, since the baby's head is pivoted assymetrically on his neck, friction with the pelvic walls produces leverage which causes him to tuck his head more tightly against his chest. This increased flexion presents the smallest and therefore the most favorable diameters to the passages.

If the final barrier, the perineum, seems too limited for the baby's head to get past, the doctor can harmlessly incise it, then stitch it back later (the operation called episiotomy). This operation, however, should be restricted to women with truly tight perineums; once it has been performed it will be necessary at subsequent births, since the scar of the first operation will never soften and stretch the way skin does.

When the baby reaches the outlet of the birth canal all the pressures are suddenly released. While steady pressures are tolerable to the human body, a sudden release such as this is both startling and painful. The baby's head should not pop out. If so, he is exposed in one shocking second to too much pressure change. Even a more gradual emergence brings the simultaneous strange experiences of outside temperature, bright, harsh light, and air. After the interior dimness of the womb, the brilliant light of the delivery room is blinding. Before delivery he was only in contact with wet things, and his airway is still filled with fluid from the uterus. Confronted with air, his mouth half full of fluid, he coughs and gasps.

Babies are born protesting their birth, and resisting it with every means at their command. The newborn baby's arms and legs wave about. His blood pressure and temperature soar. As soon as he gets some air into his lungs, he sets up the loud cry of distress.

When he emerges into the outer world, the newborn is tired, badly hurt, often temporarily scarred. The last thing in the world this weary battler needs is a slap on the back or a dash of cold water in his face (unless, of course, he is deeply anaesthetized and must be revived). It would be like taking a hose to or beating a fighter who was already down on his knees. Of course the baby's mouth and nose must be cleared out—but gently. If he has trouble breathing, the airway should be cleared by means of a very gentle method similar to mouth-to-mouth resuscitation on a small scale, just as one would do for someone who had drowned in sea water.

Sometimes the membranes do not rupture and the baby is born with his membrane still draped around him, as though he had been delivered wrapped in plastic. An old folk legend maintains that babies who are born "with the caul" over their faces will never drown at sea. The truth behind this superstition, so far as we can figure it out, may lie in the fact that if the doctor or attendant does not rupture the membrane and tear it free from the baby's face immediately so that the infant can breathe, he may never live to drown at sea!

All babies are born with a condition which, if it persisted, would be considered a congenital heart abnormality. The newborn baby literally has a hole in his heart —an open communication between the aorta, the large artery that originates in the left ventrical, and the pulmonary artery, which is on the right side of the heart.

In the adult, the two sides of the heart are different, in both strength and pressure. The right side is subject only to low pressure, since it receives blood at low pressure from the veins and pumps it into the lungs. The left side, which is stronger than the right, takes blood in at low pressure from the lungs, but then it pumps the blood up to high pressure for arterial flow.

Neither of these conditions obtains with the newborn baby. The sides of his heart are parallel and equal in both strength and pressure. They both work under the same high-pressure system. Since there is no pressure change between the two sides, the open channel, necessary before birth, now closes off, so far as function is concerned, within a few hours or a few days following birth. Anatomically, however, the hole does not close over until the baby is from one to three weeks old. That is why, when very tiny babies are crying fiercely, they may turn blue. The pressure has gone up so high that the blood leaks through the still-open hole in the heart, instead of flowing into the lungs. While frightening to new parents, this phenomenon of the newborn is actually harmless.

It has been long argued that the newborn baby's brain and memory are not developed, else he would be able to recall the agony of his birth. Memory, however, depends upon association. Birth is an unprecedented experience for the baby, unrelated to anything that he has known before, or probably will ever know in the future. He remembers it well enough that he does not want it to happen again. If you tried to put the baby through the same experience the day after he was born, he would resist violently. This time he would know enough to relate the experience to a previous unpleasant one, and he would fight with all his power.

It is easy to prove that a baby remembers the birth pain. If something very tight is forced over the head of a new-born baby, he will fight, flaying out with his tiny arms, wriggling his whole body, and crying loudly with distress, just as he did at his birth. He wants no more restricting orifices to navigate.

When he has been medically checked and found to be sound in the delivery room, the very kindest thing that can be done for the battered, weary little newborn is to give him a warm cuddling and reassurance as quickly as possible—rather than jamming him tight in a cot and telling him to cry his head off. It is artificial and unnecessary to "protect" the newborn from bacteria (unless he is premature) by isolating him in an antiseptic nursery, away from his mother's germs and emotions. The newborn must get harmless bacteria all over his skin surface as soon as possible if he is to survive this germ-filled world. He also needs to be exposed to his first pleasurable emotion. Ideally his exposure into an entirely new world—the world of feeling—should come from his mother. In our hospital, if the mother is in a good emotional state after the delivery, we give her baby to her for a quick cuddle, and then the mother and the baby are both asked to rest and sleep off the whole exhausting business. Before we put this relatively recent program into effect, both newborn babies and their mothers frequently cried following the birth. Now our mothers do not cry at all and the babies cry far less. In a hospital in Bangkok, Thailand, that allowed the mothers to have their newborn babies on little pads beside them in their own beds, from birth, my husband walked through a 380-bed maternity hospital without hearing a single cry.

After the trauma of birth, the newborn sleeps. Little babies and small children have this wonderful capacity to sleep following hurt or ill. They are unworried by what tomorrow may bring, unworried by the thought that they may be missing a whole day of life. Comforted and warm, the newborn sleeps for an entire day, perhaps even two days, rarely wakening, and when awake, is readily comforted.

chapter nine

SURVIVOR OF THE STORM
Why the Newborn Looks as He Does

The newborn baby that appears in excellent condition to the obstetrician may be a far from reassuring sight to new parents who have never before examined a tiny infant. In ante-natal classes at our hospital, I like to show expectant mothers a one-week-old newborn from the nursery, since the week-old baby is usually the same size and weight as he was at birth. In the first few days following birth, when he is tired and not eating, the baby's weight drops, and then, as he begins to eat, he picks up the weight he lost. We expect healthy newborns to weigh the same at seven days of age as they did at birth. After that, they gain between five and ten ounces each week.

The first thing one notices about the newborn is that he is not "pink and white" and decked in frilly nylon as sentimental drawings and baby food advertisements might have us believe. The skin of the newborn baby is apt to be a rich, dusky color due to the large quantities of blood which have stored up in the last few weeks before birth. When the baby cries, the color deepens to beet-red. Sometimes the blood breaks down to produce a yellowish staining of the skin after two or three days, which may appear alarming but does not persist long.

The baby's head seems to be so very large in proportion to his body that when you lift the newborn it's almost invariably a surprise to find how light he feels. In the baby's large, bony skull, the junctions are still pliable and the bony areas fit loosely together like a jigsaw puzzle. The sections of the adult skull are so tightly locked that one cannot feel any juncture between them, although the skull is made up of six separate bony areas.

The newborn baby's skull is open and unjoined so that he could tolerate deformation during birth. The bony sections can telescope in the baby's head without causing permanent injury. Most all babies are born with some skull deformation, but the skull springs back into shape shortly after birth. One reason that doctors always hope for a slow rather than swift delivery is that the skull tolerates a slow deformation much better than it does a rapid one. If the baby's skull is expelled too swiftly and the pressures are too intense, there is a risk of tearing of blood vessels inside.

If one places ones fingertips gently on the baby's head one can feel in both the front and back of the skull where the five bones come together, two soft depressions, the fontanelles. They have no bone over them as yet, and are covered only by a layer of tough membrane. On the baby's head, the pulse beats visibly under the skin in the fontanelles. When the baby cries, the membrane covering may bulge out a little—just as when adults cry or scream the veins in their faces stand out. This is quite harmless for the baby, since the covering is much stronger than it looks, and the baby's scalp can be washed with no danger of hurting his head.

This extreme plasticity and adaptability of the new-born's skull is one of the marvels of birth. If an x-ray of an unborn baby, or of an adult, showed the bones of the skull overlapping, it would most certainly indicate that the individual was dead. Yet the bones of the baby's skull, during birth, frequently overlap, and they slip back in place when the ordeal is over with no permanent damage. The posterior fontanelle, the smaller one in the back of the head, usually closes up by the age of six months. It takes the larger fontanelle in the front of the skull another nine months to close entirely.

The scalp of the newborn's head, which is soft tissue, may be quite swollen at birth because of the compression behind it. Fortunately, most babies are born with their chins tucked down and their faces well protected, so that the only swelling is in the scalp on top of their heads. A few less lucky infants are delivered face first, in which case they appear to have been in a fight, with their faces puffed and badly bruised. This sort of swelling, on either scalp or face, means little to the obstetrician, who knows that the newborn is rapidly self-healing (much more so than an adult would be). But the thoughtful doctor will explain to the mother and her husband that this is an entirely reversible phenomenon which, no matter how shocking it appears, will disappear within days. Some nurses may feel it's better to hide the baby if he looks like this, but if the mother reassures the nurse that she understands the temporary condition, she will bring the baby out.

The lower face of the newborn seems quite small and underdeveloped in relation to the large skull, because the facial bones are not nearly so developed as is the vault of the skull. The jaw of the newborn appears undershot, giving the baby a chinless look. This is quite an asset in feeding since it enables the baby to nurse without the handicap of a jawbone between his lips and the food supply. When the newborn opens his mouth, there is a thin fold of tissue attached under the tip of the tongue. This is sometimes mistaken for the tongue-tied condition, but as the baby grows, the attachment recedes further back in the mouth.

The eyeballs, like the auditory system of the newborn, are nearly adult in size, and therefore are apt to seem too close together. The Japanese recognize this phenomenon by designing their dolls with adult-sized eyes in baby faces. This also explains why so many babies and small children have such a "wide-eyed" expression, which they lose when the rest of their facial features catch up with the development of their eyes.

If the newborn was premature, he is apt to resemble an extremely wrinkled old person, since he shares with the aged a lack of subcutaneous fat. On both, the tiny preemie and the very old person, the layer of fat that normally lies just beneath the skin is thin or missing, so that the features are wrinkled and drawn rather than rounded or smooth.

Mothers often quite wrongly suffer feelings of guilt if they discover any birthmark on their baby's skin, fearing that they did something wrong during pregnancy. In New Zealand, if the baby has a "strawberry stain" the mother is convinced it's because she was a glutton during the berry season. It is sometimes quite difficult to dissuade her from such an old wives' tale. Strawberry marks, a local malformation of the blood vessels in the skin, appear raised like a strawberry and gradually develop small white specks of skin on them. They will eventually disappear, although some may persist until school age. Port wine stains, which look like red dye spilled onto the skin, remain for life unless they are treated by cosmetic surgery. Coffee-colored marks and blue streaks are the result of some abnormality of pigmentation. Occasionally a newborn, especially among the darker races, has blue spots on his lower back or buttocks, like a fox terrier; this is known medically as Mongolian spots (not to be confused with mongolism), which usually decrease in size or completely disappear very early in life. All babies are born relatively fair, and as the general pigmentation develops the spots fade into the overall skin color. Moles and hairy spots rarely are present at birth but start appearing in babyhood and increase throughout childhood.

Birthmarks have nothing to do with the mother's behavior during pregnancy, and usually nothing needs to be done about them, since most disappear in time. If a birthmark remains which might affect the child's appearance, it can be treated as any minor cosmetic defect. After the spot has healed, plastic surgery can be performed when convenient. Harelips, which occur during the baby's developmental stage, can be corrected by cosmetic surgery while the child is still small. The occasional marks that are left by doctors' instruments during difficult deliveries seldom remain long, since the newborn heals so very quickly.

Although the baby can see when he is born, the womb was a shapeless environment and he knows nothing about size and shape. Even the contours of his mother's face must be learned—a lesson which usually takes the newborn several weeks. While there was sufficient stimulation within the womb for him to learn to differentiate between light and dark, all the rest that constitutes total vision must still be learned. In addition to the shape of things, he must learn color and the physical use of the eyes. It is not unusual to see one of the tiny baby's eyes go off in one direction, and the other in the opposite direction. This "squinty" or "cross-eyed" look can be alarming unless one knows that for the first few weeks of his life the newborn has not yet mastered binocular vision. It will take him a while to learn how to focus his eyes, and then he must learn how to make them work together in the same direction.

The newborn's elasticity of bones and ligaments makes it possible to correct quite easily irregularities that may have been caused by his cramped position in late pregnancy. Some newborn babies' feet were so cramped that they will not bend straight up and straight down. While the newborn is still so very pliable, however, the foot can be worked and massaged to increase its flexibility, with no fear of breaking the leg. The father can do this when he is playing with his baby. He can gently massage the foot muscles each time he fondles the baby, until he sees that the infant has his full range of movement.

Similarly the baby's neck muscles may have been affected by his position in the womb. If he was lying, during the final weeks of pregnancy, with his head tucked down on one side all the time, the muscles on that side may be somewhat shorter than those on the other side. The baby's head can be rotated gently to exercise the neck muscles. And when he is lying in his crib, a stack of folded diapers can be placed under the deficient side, then one removed from the pile each week until the muscular development seems equal on both sides.

In late pregnancy there is a final acceleration of hormone production which is equivalent, in its effects on the baby's body, to adolescence. The newborn baby's external sex organs, the genitalia and the breasts, swell. And the breasts of both boy and girl babies may secrete some milk —known as "witches' milk." Occasionally newborn girls show a slight menstrual flow for a few days following their birth.

Still another hormonal reaction that is common to both sexes is the familiar red spots on newborn babies' skin which are politely referred to as "baby rash." Pharmaceutical companies have made fortunes with medicants to treat baby rash, since conscientious mothers want to "do something" about it. As a matter of fact, this rash is a form of non-scarring adolescent acne which is transient, harmless, and will disappear with or without medication. If infection should set in, however, it should be treated with an antibiotic cream.

The first time she sees her newborn baby naked, the mother will notice a little stump of cord left at the navel. This slowly shrivels and drops off after a few days, leaving a little moist patch of thin skin which will eventually contract into scar tissue. Around this patch is a cuff of skin which will turn in as the child's abdominal shape flattens with growth. The navel changes slowly from the popped-out button on the protuberant abdomen of the newborn to the slightly indented navel on the still-protuberant abdomen of a child, and finally to the marked inversion of the navel of the model adult. The navel has been a subject for suspicion and witchcraft among various peoples at different times in our history. One form of modern witchcraft that I have seen is the practice of binding a baby's navel, sometimes with a coin to cover the navel itself. To attain a model inverted navel, all the baby really needs to do is to grow into a nice strong little chap with an abdominal wall that flattens out as he grows.

As the newborn baby sleeps—which he does most of the time for the first few days—only the top of his head may be visible. It is important to keep the baby warm, so that he is usually tucked in firmly. He is unlikely to resist this in the early days unless he is lying on and squashing his own arm. It should not be tucked under him. As he grows older, however, and spends more of his time each day lying awake, the baby no longer seems to want that sensation of being tucked in firmly. By the time he is two or three weeks old, the newborn baby wants to have his hands, and possibly his feet, free.

Probably the greatest single change the newborn encounters when he first emerges into the strange outer world is gravity. In the womb he remained buoyant even during those final cramped stages. Following his birth, however, the newborn finds himself in a position somewhat similar to that of the astronaut who has just come off a space flight, and must adjust from weightlessness to gravity. The baby is no longer buoyant, and blood may not circulate well in his extremities. He has difficulty in stabilizing his blood pressure.

When he is lying flat, everything that is raised from that position demands that he work against gravity. Since the newborn baby's head is so very large and heavy in relation to the remainder of his body, he will lift it last—after he has mastered the problem of raising an arm or a leg. It is because of this relative weight of the head that the one cardinal rule for handling the newborn is to make certain that his head is supported and not allowed to dangle. The baby cannot hold up his head by himself.

chapter ten

FIRST LESSON IN LOVE
Handling the Newborn

One shouldn't be afraid to handle the newborn baby. He is actually an astonishingly tough little creature. He can withstand surgery that would lay low a strong adult. Physiologically he is a remarkably strong and durable animal; his ligaments and bones are still pliant and elastic, so there is little chance of bone breakage. He is far from fragile, and there is really no reason not to handle him, unless a head injury is suspected.

On the contrary, the newborn needs to be handled. For this is his introduction to human contact, communication, and love. It is at this time, when he is first born, that the baby is most strongly influenced emotionally by his mother. Having had no emotional communication within the uterus, he will "catch" the first emotions that fall his way, and soak them up like a piece of blotting paper. It is up to his mother to fill him with love and reassurance so that he will have a good start at life and at relations with other people.

When the mother takes her newborn baby into her arms for the first time after his birth, and soothes and comforts him, her baby is receiving his first lesson in the emotion of comforting love. Within the first three days of his extra-uterine life he is destined to experience three new emotions: the comfort of his mother's arms, the distress of hunger, and the pleasure of nourishment.

Immediately following birth, the baby is too exhausted to feel hunger. It takes him several days of rest to get over the experience of birth. Usually the time his hunger becomes distressing coincides with the time the mother's milk comes in, on about the third day after birth. While she does not yet have milk, however, the first day or two offer a nice time for the mother and baby to get acquainted through a few practice feeding sessions. Mothers whose first attempt at nursing their babies comes when a nurse hands them the baby and says, "It's feed time; here is your baby," are apt to be upset and nervous. These tensions are transmitted to the baby and make him nervous too, so that feeding may not be very successful the first two or three times.

Both the baby and the mother can do with some practice before they begin the serious business of regular feedings. Although the newborn does know how to use his mouth to suck and swallow—and most full-term babies have a very strong suck—he still does not know about the nipple or the breast. And, unless she's had other babies, the mother, too, is an amateur at feeding. If the baby is left alone with the mother, she can put him to her breast, hold him, and get used to the feel of him. He in turn can grow accustomed, through a few such trial sessions, to finding out about her, how to be comfortable against her body, and how to find her nipple to suckle. In these trial runs, the baby should be put to each breast for only one minute, three or four times within the twenty-four hours. Then he is offered glucose and water and tucked up to sleep again.

After the mother's milk comes in, she has plenty of opportunity to handle and hold her child. One of the reasons I so strongly recommend breast feeding is that it provides the newborn the greatest reassurance that he can have at this early stage of life: a continuity of handling. Each time he experiences the pain of hunger it is his mother, the same person, who answers his needs. Nurses, no matter how kind and loving with babies, work on eight-hour shifts. That means that the newborn who is entirely fed by bottle will probably be handled and fed by two or three different women within a twenty-four-hour period. He may be brought to his own mother, for her to hold and feed him, for only some of his feeding periods.

While the newborn baby does not yet distinguish adults by sight, he does know them by their tempo, the way in which they hold him, the way they move—whether they are languid or brusque—just as he learned the feel of his mother's movements while he was in the womb. Babies know very clearly whether they are being handled by someone who is confident or someone who is nervous; and it is only when he is very distressed that a newborn will not settle when held with confidence.

It was once thought that because the baby was accustomed to living in cramped quarters during the final few weeks of his intra-uterine life, it should be reassuring for him to be wrapped with the crib sheets tucked in tightly around him all the time. Now we know that after the first 2 or 3 days babies have natural "wake periods" when to be tightly bound in the crib and left alone to cry is the most miserable way to be. The reassurance the newborn baby needs most is the kind that comes from the nearness of another human body: body heat, the gentle monotony of the heartbeat, the warmth of adult arms. The human baby gets reassurance from his mother in much the same way that young lambs or foals or calves do, from the sense of physical nearness and gentle handling.

When babies are going to be given up for adoption, the rule often is that the mother never sees or handles the baby, supposedly making the emotional trauma easier for her. But it is harder for the baby. Prolonged lack of emotional communication may leave a lifelong impression. Studies have shown us that if a human baby, or a puppy, or a baby monkey is isolated at this early stage, and not provided the reassurance and feeling that comes from handling and closeness to another body, it becomes hostile and finds it difficult—if not impossible—to develop good relationships with others in later life. It becomes a born hermit.

We have also found through such studies that the babies who are handled and brought up by several different people are much more likely to be disturbed than those who are so fortunate as to be brought up by one person. The former babies cry a lot more; they don't settle down and go to sleep as easily. Nearness to a single person, whom they quickly recognize by the way in which that person handles them, seems to be very important to the reassurance of the tiny infant. Since human development depends so largely on learning from others, a born hermit will restrict himself intellectually as well as emotionally.

If the baby's mother will look after him at home, she is the logical person to handle him most in the hospital. Undoubtedly many children have grown up happily tended by nannies. But these nannies were experts at reassurance, took over the babies at an early age, and provided them the continuity of handling that they needed, acting in effect as the substitute mother.

The newborn's need for this sort of physical reassurance is due in a large part to the kind of animal he is. Newborn mammals are divided into three types. The nesting types, such as kittens and puppies, are born in a very immature state and nuzzle together in a nest where their mother comes to tend them. The "grazing" types such as cows and lambs, who are born with four props on which to stand upright within hours after birth, can get around by themselves quite well. They are, of course, born in a rather more mature state than the multiple offspring of cats and dogs.

Human babies, as well as other primates, fall into a third category: the clinging types. Their maturity at birth is intermediate between the nesting and grazing mammals. They instinctively cling to their mothers tightly with their hands. If a small baby hears someone stamp on the floor loudly or senses that he might be dropped, he will grab and grasp tightly at the throat or breast of the person who is holding him. What he may be really reaching for is long hair to cling to. My children broke innumerable strings of beads with that instinctive clinging gesture. If women really wanted to provide the maximum reassurance for very small babies, they would wear their hair hanging down long in front where the baby could grasp it. Instead, most mothers "put it up," out of the way of little hands.

If the baby had his way, his mother would also carry him around wherever she went, as the other primates do. They have their babies attached to them, clinging to their hair, from birth. The mothers keep their babies warm that way. Of course, even if she wanted to please the baby, the human mother's domestic duties and social life wouldn't allow it. She would never get her marketing or her housework done, or be able to go out with her husband in the evening. But the baby would be happy. Some of the world's happiest babies live on islands in temperate climates, where the mother's warm body is partially bare, her long hair in easy reach, and her baby slung across one hip or tied to her back.

Fortunately for us all, the human being has very little instinct left. We wouldn't know how to migrate like birds, for example, or form hives as bees do. In fact, to compare human beings to birds and bees is quite ridiculous. Aside from the strong clinging gesture, the newborn has little instinctive behavior to limit his learning. His mind is open and free to absorb all new things, and he is also delightfully impervious to failure. If, as is true with adults, a failure represented humiliation, guilt, or self-consciousness, the newborn's rate of learning would be immeasurably slowed down; having made one error, he would hesitate to expose himself to ridicule again. The newborn, however, has no such nonsense to impede his development, and his rate of learning, in his waking periods, is phenomenal. As soon as he is rested up from the ordeal of birth, he eagerly tackles the many things he must learn.

The newborn's comfort, internal and external, continues to mean a great deal to him for many weeks. But now he is able to communicate his feelings to listening ears. There are those who say that babies are not interesting until they learn how to talk. But those who say this have simply not taken the trouble to learn the infant's language. The small baby learns to understand many things about adults long before he can handle words. And for adults to assume that the child is not communicating until he can use words is like saying that all foreigners are crazy because they don't speak English. The baby has his own ways of communicating, and it is up to the adults to learn to understand them. This is still another reason why second babies so often seem far easier to handle than first babies do; the mother has "tuned in" on the infant world, and learned how to communicate with her baby.

An adult's ability to communicate well with other adults will prove of little help in learning to communicate with an infant. The newborn has had no opportunity to learn to communicate in adult terms. Speech will take a long time to develop. Competence at seeing takes time to develop. If the newborn can't see clearly whom he is talking to, he cannot learn to use the facial expressions and other reactions with which adults communicate.

The newborn communicates with his entire body. There are, as yet, no fine gradations to his feelings, which in themselves are quite new. He is either totally happy or totally unhappy. If he is happy, he will clench his toes or fan them in an overall surge of pleasure, or just sleep. When he is unhappy, he cries, not just with his face, but with his entire body.

While the newborn may not appear to comprehend what the adult is doing or saying, by showing any response with which the adult is familiar, the baby is by no means insensitive to his surroundings or to what is going on. It is useless to expect a recognizable response from a very small baby. Some adults mistakenly torment tiny babies by trying to provoke an identifiable response from them. They will jiggle the newborn baby up and down and tickle him mercilessly, in the hope of inducing a nice big smile or a gurgle of laughter. It has been stated that the infant does not smile before he is five or six weeks of age, but, in fact, babies do often smile when they are much younger than that. Smiling seems to be a sort of experiment at first, but as their vision improves they may imitate the smile that they see on the adult face.

The mother is very likely to get one of her first pleasurable responses from her baby when she is bathing him. If she is very careful to make certain that the bath is pleasant—with the water neither too cool nor too hot—and if she holds the baby carefully so that there is no chance of his slipping and becoming frightened, he will enjoy his bath very much. He knows the feeling of fluid around his body, and immersion in water again gives him a brief respite from his fight against gravity. He is buoyant once more, and like polio victims, he has a full range of movement with the aid of the water which he does not yet have when he is outside it.

It is up to each mother to learn to cope with and communicate with her baby. No two babies are alike, not even siblings. What worked very well with one baby may not necessarily prove successful with the next one. The mother must learn about each baby and modify her handling to suit his particular needs and personality. I had handled two babies, and felt myself certainly experienced at such simple procedures as feeding and bathing babies, when I had my third child. He was such a great big baby and grew so fast that all too soon he simply would not fit into the baby bath where I had bathed his older brother and sister. In the end, I simply put him in the big tub with them, a procedure which all three seemed to enjoy enormously.

Rules, Oscar Wilde remarked, were made "for the guidance of wise men and the confusion of fools." Probably no human experience will equal the care of an infant for teaching that one must be prepared at all times to modify rules.

chapter eleven

HE HAS HIS OWN LANGUAGE
A Key to Crying

Nothing distresses a conscientious mother more than the sound of her baby's crying. She must go and attend to him at once, or suffer an excited state that makes her inefficient, or become frankly irritable. Her peace of mind depends on finding out what the crying means.

The newborn's cry has no definition as speech. Although each baby will have a different cry, according to the shape of the resonating parts of his mouth and pharynx, he will always cry the same way at first. The sound is made by blowing air out of the larynx across the vocal cords. Unborn babies can make crying movements, but unless air is present in the womb no sound is heard. Premature babies cry, and newborns are capable of producing a very lusty sound.

At one time a great deal of importance was attached to a high-pitched, shrill cry, which was said to indicate brain damage. While any such unusual cry should be investigated, doctors are now looking to other factors for abnormality and brain damage. Still a lusty cry at birth is the best possible indication that all is well.

The baby's condition at birth may well parallel that of his mother. If she has had a difficult time, he will also. If she is in a stupor from medication, he also is sleepy from the relatively large amount of anaesthetic he received. A baby breathes and cries most readily if his mother is awake, well, and co-operating in his birth.

The first breaths of air are hard work for the newborn baby. His airways are still full of fluid, and the alveoli, the tiny thin-walled air sacs in the lungs, have to be blown up like so many thousand microscopic balloons. Fortunately the lungs do not have to inflate completely right away, and the absorption of fluid into the extra-cellular spaces and the expansion of air sacs goes on as a continuous process over the first weeks of the newborn's life. Premature babies work on a relatively small amount of inflated lung and thus are much more vulnerable if foreign material such as milk or mucous is inhaled into the airways.

Many theories have been advanced as to why a baby makes vigorous breathing movements with crying at birth. Investigations have measured the levels of oxygen and carbon dioxide in the baby's cord blood at birth. There has been much philosophizing on the effects of the sudden temperature drop, the gravitational change, and the effect of first handling. Certainly there is no correlation between the amounts of oxygen or carbon dioxide a baby has and the latency of the newborn's breathing and crying response—unless one considers the nearly terminal gasping of a dangerously ill baby. There seems no better explanation for birth cries than that they are an expression of the baby's discomfort. We know the baby can make similar movements before he ever enters the birth passages, if he is distressed in the womb, and can make sounds which are audible if air is present. We also know that no form of birth is easy for the baby. Even a Caesarian means a very sudden change from warmth, darkness, and relative quiet to the rough hands and bright lights of the operating room.

The baby is born protesting this discomfort in the only way he knows—by sucking air in and blasting it out again. Breathing and crying are part of one act. Following the initial birth cries, the newly born baby falls into a very deep sleep from which it is hard to arouse him, whether the mother has had any medication or not. This is to be expected, after the loss of sleep he sustained during labor. In our studies we found that eighty percent of babies awoke and emitted sustained crying only twice within their first twenty-four hours following birth. However, one can observe babies whimpering in their sleep. Presumably they are either too sleepy or not sufficiently uncomfortable to reach consciousness.

The baby's first cries—over the first days and weeks— are a reflex response to discomfort. Eventually he will use his voice to indicate many different feelings, demands, and communications. But the progress from that early all-purpose cry to the much more refined cry of the older child, who in his screwed-up, tearful face is expressing a definite emotion, is rather slow. The infant's cry is a general bodily reaction. He cries all over. There is the piercing "waanh waah" cry of distress which in itself has a very different sound from the older child's emotional, heartbroken sobbing. The baby's arms and legs thrash about. His blood pressure and body temperature shoot up, and he gets that red, hard-boiled look. All in all, the newborn manages to both sound and look quite fierce.

By the third day of life, by far the most common cause of crying is hunger, which is very distressing to the new-

*Even at two or three he is still talking
(communicating) with his whole body.*

born. There is a definite rhythm to this sort of discomfort, probably related to the baby's own inherent sleep rhythm, which, like the adult's, varies between deep and light sleep. Unlike adults, however, the baby's sleep pattern at this stage is not yet diurnal (active by day, sleeping at night), and the newborn will sleep and wake at fairly regular intervals around the clock. When he is sleeping lightly all types of stimuli will be perceived at a much lower threshold than with an older child or adult. Adults have learned to exert some conscious control over what they feel and the threshold of stimulus at which they feel it. In addition, the adult brain has so many stimuli to deal with that many sensations never reach it. Most women have experienced the frustration of trying to get a reply out of their husband when he is deeply absorbed in a book or a ball game. He just does not hear. The baby has no such handy ability to shut out sensation. His brain receives all stimuli indiscriminately. Furthermore, the baby's tender skin, fresh taste buds, acute ears, and sensitive stomach alert him to distress that adults would barely notice. This was proved rather dramatically recently by a doctor and his team, working in a New York hospital, who devised a method of detecting brain-damaged babies by giving them a standardized little flip with a rubber band on the heel. When this same flip was applied to the tenderest parts of the adult anatomy, the adult was barely aware of it, and felt no pain. Yet the flip on the heel of a normal newborn was a powerful enough sensation to evoke loud, persistent squalling, even if the infant was sleeping lightly.

After a period the hunger-pang-cry-feeding-comfort sequence becomes a conditioned reflex for the normal baby. This is the beginning of his conscious use of vocalization to communicate. His crying is approaching a form of speech. At first the baby cries with any sort of discomfort, but if he is gently cared for, hunger soon becomes the principal and recurring stimulus. He cries; his mother feeds him; he is comforted. Eventually, depending on his own innate ability to associate ideas in his brain, he will realize that his cry, not his hunger, brings his mother, and in time his cry will become a purposeful act. He will learn to vary his cry to mean different things and his mother will be doing her best to interpret his meaning. Some of his sounds will make her laugh at him or cuddle him; others will elicit her anxiety and distress. It is a two-way act, the beginning of speech. This early communication is actually a far more important milestone in the baby's life than when he cuts his first tooth.

Babies, it can safely be said, never cry for fun. The most effective way to turn a baby into a non-communicative introvert is to ignore his cry. In studies of maternal deprivation, one can see the effects of breaking the cry-feed-comfort cycle most dramatically with a lamb. The lamb is born at a more mature stage, and having a relatively short life cycle, he exhibits the effects in a relatively short observation period. The experimental lamb is orphaned at birth and kept alive for the first few days of his life with milk from a bottle, which is provided sparingly and haphazardly, and not associated with his crying. At first the lamb will cry a great deal of the time. Intermittent hunger forces him to nibble at grass and plants, and at ten days he is able to nearly sustain himself. If he is now put out in a field with other lambs and ewes and given one milk feeding to keep him alive, he will quite rapidly become a complete hermit. If he tries to make up to some of the ewes in an effort to find a mother, he is repulsed with a sharp nudge. He has to spend his hours grazing or chewing cud. When the shepherd calls to give him a feed, which is now from a reluctant ewe instead of the bottle, the hermit lamb has to be chased down and caught. By the age of three weeks the lamb is weedy looking and completely silent. He never cries. All his attention is directed to self-preservation. He is tense when he is held, ready always to make a break. He takes what he can when he can. His only comfort is a dank little corner under a log or bush where he retires to chew or sleep. Where is that affectionate, lovable little lamb that followed Mary to school and cried for her when he was hungry? The hermit lamb has no mother figure; he is well on his way to losing all ability to make normal sheep relationships.

For forty years, until a decade ago, many doctors and nurses advised that babies should be left to cry. They based this advice on a completely false premise: that babies suffered severe gastroenteric disease and even death from overfeeding. Even after this disease was finally and conclusively attributed to infection, the theory still obtained that babies should not be fed too often, and that if bottle-fed, when the likelihood of gastroenteritis was much greater, they should not have too much food. On the opposite pole of infant care, the more permissive school—promulgated by doctors who were considered complete reactionaries by the older, regularized-schedule school—reversed this theory under the able, popular pen of Dr. Benjamin Spock. But the patterns of enforced regular feeding and ignoring babies' cries have been perpetuated in hospital nurseries, orphanages, and, unfortunately, too many homes.

We do not know how many anxious human beings,

humorless souls, how many introverts may have grown out of the "let the baby cry" theory, any more than we can know what effect the ancient practice of killing the first-born had. The medical people who advocated crying as good for the baby at least felt that they were preventing the baby from a miserable death. They worked in good faith, as did the barber-surgeons in the blood-letting days. All one can conclude is that in some future society which values each child as worthy of a good start in life, the "let the baby cry" age will be recalled as a period of barbarism.

The obvious reason that infants cry so frequently is that this is their only means of communicating their distress. Adults have many ways of expressing discomfort or pain. They can clutch their heads or their stomachs. They can moan, scream, or wail endlessly about what ails them. But the baby has only this one means of telling everyone that something is wrong. And he uses this form of communication indiscriminately, crying whether his distress is only mild or whether he is really in pain.

Since the most common reason for the newborn to cry is hunger pain, it is only sensible to first offer him food. Babies vary a great deal both in their food needs and in their individual manner of eating. It is not unusual for light feeders to be hungry within two or three hours after they have eaten. Never assume that a baby "can't be hungry" just because he was fed recently. The times of feeding do not provide the only answer. It is best to keep a chart showing the number of times the baby has been fed in a day rather than the actual hours. Some of the gravest errors in the care of small babies have been committed in the name of feeding. One simply can't prescribe one amount or one pattern for all babies. The baby himself is the only one who can reasonably dictate how much he wants to eat. His way of measuring his hunger has nothing to do with the time of day, but is associated with his metabolic rhythm. He's had all he wants when he leaves a half ounce in the bottle or stops suckling the breast.

An infant who feeds whenever he's hungry will gain from five ounces to one pound per week. This means that the baby who could be gaining a full pound, but who is held down to a seven-ounce gain (which, according to the rule book, is "sufficient") may cry all the time because he's so hungry. I recall, a dozen years ago, being called to examine a post-mature baby, twelve pounds at birth, whose feeding was being prescribed according to a wall chart for a seven-and-a-half-pound baby. The head nurse was so distressed by this baby's constant crying that she thought he might have a hernia! He was only starving, and doing his best to let the world know it with the only means at his command.

Offering the baby the breast, even when he is not hungry, may quiet him. Many babies simply enjoy oral stimulation and find the breast or the bottle extremely soothing. Let them suckle for a while and they will peacefully slip off to sleep again, with the nipple or the teat still in their mouths.

Parents worry unduly about this sort of infant behavior, fearing that it, like thumb sucking, might be habit-forming. But allowing the infant to persist in whatever practices provide him comfort is not courting the risk of a bad habit. Neither thumb sucking nor oral stimulation of this sort is any cause for parental concern unless it persists past infancy. Most babies stop these practices when they no longer need them. And if the parents should attempt to discourage the infant by putting something bitter on his thumb or on the nipple, it will only make the baby cross and irritable. He is far too young, at this stage, to either understand or countenance efforts at discipline.

Another reason for crying that is common to all babies, and second only to hunger, is thermal discomfort. Unlike adults, newborn babies do not have a good temperature-control system and have considerable difficulty maintaining comfortable body temperature. The temperature-control device, which is located in the midbrain, was not used by the baby until after his birth. Like all delicate mechanisms, it takes a while to establish itself and attain an adult pattern of operation.

The adult body regulates temperature by cutting down heat loss from the skin, through shivering, goose pimples, and capillary constriction, when the body is cold. When the body is hot, the heat loss is increased through the dilation of the capillaries in the skin and sweating. Adults spread out in the heat, draw up and shiver in the cold, consciously and sensibly tailoring their muscles to their needs.

Newborn babies do not shiver. When they are cold they wave their arms and legs and cry to produce heat. A crying baby uses twice as much energy as a sleeping baby. If the baby's body temperature is dropping, he doubles his body heat production; this is a good thing, unlike the times he cries when he is hungry, and runs up a calorie debt in his efforts to get food.

Newborns are able to lose heat quite effectively through sweating, as they have nearly five times as many sweat glands on any given area of skin as adults have. Provided the baby is given plenty of fluid (milk and water) he can keep himself from "cooking" if his skin is bare. If he is covered in nylon or swaddled, this ability is immediately destroyed. Heat and overheating are far more dangerous to a human being than cold; the former can cause brain damage and death, while the worst effects of cooling are slowing of growth, generalized weight loss, and raised blood pressure from the extra activity required to keep warm.

A mother should try to put herself in the baby's place and then make a sensible decision about his comfort. She should remember that plastics and nylons hold in heat and can be very irritating. The baby should be dressed for the prevailing temperature, and one should be conscious of sudden changes in temperature. What is the outside air like compared to the air inside the house? The first time the newborn is due for a sharp change is when he is taken home from the hospital. The mother should consider what the outdoor temperature is compared to the hospital nursery.

While most mothers remember to wrap up a baby against cold weather, they are less likely to consider their baby's reaction to heat, which is more important.

A baby does not need much clothing at any time. Due to his metabolic rate, he has a very high level of heat production, and he is always in danger of being overheated. It is customary to overdress babies in warm weather. Part of this, I suppose, is due to the vanity of grannies and the mothers who want their baby to "look pretty," and doll him up in dresses and boots that only itch and irritate him. The baby's method of dissipating heat is not functioning the way the adult's does. He needs to have his face and head shaded from the sun, but his body, in hot weather, should be as open to the air as possible for free evaporation of sweat. In hot weather all the baby needs is the diapers and a large sun hat; this is preferable to having to cope with overheated babies who may cry, vomit, or even convulse.

Because the small baby has difficulty in regulating his body temperature, doctors are concerned with fever in infants. Although fever in itself is only a symptom, a small baby's fever may be more dangerous than the disease. If an infant runs a high fever, the doctor usually works to control and reduce the fever before he does anything else, since there is a possibility of damage, especially to the brain. The commonest cause of convulsions in an infant— which is probably the most terrifying sight a new mother can observe—is not epilepsy, as so many used to think, but fever from infections of the ear or throat. Fortunately, this type of convulsion does not persist. The older child or adult developing a fever has a rigor, the infant or newborn a convulsion.

When a baby is sick, one should not pile on gowns or bedclothes to keep him warm, or turn up the thermostat so that he is lying in a hot room. Heat is of no help in treating infant disorders. If the baby feels hot to the touch, one can help him control his temperature by stimulating a little artificial "sweating" for him, by bathing his skin with a tepid washcloth.

Babies do not persist in their crying for no reason. But different babies do cry for different reasons. If the baby is not hungry and seems neither too hot nor too cold, one should check for irritants, such as a diaper pin that might have opened. Or, if the baby is wearing mittens or boots, a thread inside might have pulled tight and be catching his tender fingers or toes. Some babies cry when they feel the temporary abdominal discomfort that comes from being too full. Sometimes, if this is what's bothering the baby, he will pull his legs up over his abdomen to give a clue.

After a mother has watched her baby awhile, she will soon recognize his individual pattern. Often babies cry just before they empty their bladders or their bowels. A baby boy with a full bladder often sustains an erection of the penis, a sign at this stage that he is uncomfortable. Most all babies cry if they are frightened—or merely lonely. This is when proximity to another human body comforts them. The father can hold and comfort the baby quite as well as the mother. Even when they have nothing in particular bothering them, small babies often just want to be held. Like the small child who appears at his parents' bedroom door and wants to "get in with Mummy and Daddy" in the middle of the night, he feels lonely and wants to touch his parents.

One of the most overlooked causes for babies' crying is sheer boredom. The bored cry is usually a loud, protesting wail, which marvelously stops, mid-note, when the baby is picked up. The baby is in one of his waking periods and has nothing to do. No one has come to visit him, and he has nothing to look at, so he cries for attention. Although mothers can't carry their babies around every time they are awake, it is considerate to try to bring the baby into the center of household activity so that he can see what's going on. He can be propped into a portable infant seat, and put in the kitchen where the other children are having their lunch, or be set on the table to watch his mother cook supper. I remember one very conscientious older mother who had just had her first baby home a few days when he set up a terrible clamor one Sunday morning, while she and her husband were dawdling over late breakfast and the newspapers. She checked everything that could possibly be wrong with the baby, but to no avail. Finally, out of desperation, she brought him back to the kitchen table. The moment he was part of the family group, with something to look at, he was content.

Most crying does not signify anything seriously wrong. As a mother learns her baby's own patterns and requirements, she learns how to console him. She offers him food, picks him up, holds him. She checks things that might be causing him irritation. If it is impossible to keep on holding him, he can be offered something near his mouth to nuzzle, suck on, or cling to. Very often Granny or some friend will have given him a wooly toy that he enjoys, or perhaps he's satisfied with the corner of a soft blanket. Very often the baby will fasten onto one object which becomes his special "cuddly," and he won't go to sleep without it.

Babies learn to grasp at things very early. Hold a finger close to a small baby's face where he can see it clearly. He will grasp onto it with surprising strength. Often he is able to pull himself up into a sitting position by clinging to his mother's finger, long before he can actually sit up unaided.

All of my babies had this very strong clinging instinct, and I gave them something soft to cling to and hold near their faces in the crib. Since a favored stuffed animal will get dirtier and dirtier as the weeks go by, I found the most practical "cuddly" was a soft, clean diaper. When the baby was sleeping I could slip the used diaper away and replace it with a fresh one, without his being the wiser. They were all made of the same, soft material and felt identical to the baby.

The baby's desire to hold something soft in his hand and

near his face is very strong instinctive behavior which somehow fits into his overall emotional setup. An infant whose hands are tightly bound down in his crib can get very unhappy in his wakeful moments simply because he has nothing to cling to.

Only about one tenth of all newborn babies, including premature babies as well as full-term ones, shed tears—which seems curious, when one considers that the newborn produces other fluids, such as urine, saliva, and sweat, four times as much per unit of body mass as do adults (in a cool climate). Tears will come soon, however, and usually by the fifth or sixth week of age most babies can produce tears—as well as a beautiful smile.

Crying is the first sound the baby makes. Since it is his only form of communication at this stage of his life, he comes to use it with varying intensity to indicate different things: hunger, pain, boredom. Of all the young baby's cries, the hunger cry is usually the most frequent, demanding, and persistent. The baby's "sick" cry is often little more than a low wail or whimper. Pain provokes a sharp, high cry of unmistakable distress. When the baby is overheated and overclothed, he is most likely to sound angry and fretful. As a mother gets to know her baby better, day by day, she will find that she is soon able to differentiate among his varying cries, just as a naturalist learns to distinguish bird calls and tell a mating song from a note of warning.

The more a mother listens to her baby, the better tuned she will become to what precisely he is trying to say. She will find that her anxiety decreases in proportion to her new understanding of his cries.

chapter twelve

BABY'S BEST TOOL
What His Mouth Means to Him

The part of his body with which the small baby is most familiar is his mouth and the area of his face immediately surrounding the mouth, which is called the circumoral area. The newborn can feel temperature, pain, touch, and pressure over his entire body surface. But since many of these sensations are quite new to him, his brain cannot yet sort them all out, interpret them, and localize them.

The newborn has become acquainted with his mouth and its uses through a combination of instinct and experience. His suckling instinct, which was active months before his birth, has given him control of the mechanics of sucking and swallowing. He also has a strong seeking or rooting instinct. When the newborn is given his first medical examination following birth, if the doctor pinches or pricks his toe or his bottom, the baby will react to the prick, and register protest by flaying out his arms, wriggling his body, and perhaps crying. He knows that he's been hurt, and he is conscious of the pain. But he does not know what hurt him. Nor could he put his finger on the spot that was pricked. He is quite as likely to move toward the thing that hurt him as he is to draw away from it. Except for the area of his face immediately adjacent to his mouth, the baby's sensations cannot yet be localized.

When the examining physician lays a finger along the cheek of the newborn, however, the baby turns toward the finger. He knows perfectly well that he has a mouth, and he knows where it is and how to use it. He is ready to suckle. His movement is guided by instinct and a good deal of previous intra-uterine experience.

All learning depends on experience. At first, most of his skin sensations, which are all quite new to the newborn baby, produce no more than a blurry image on his conscious mind because he has had no experience with which to relate them. It takes a good while for the "nearly new" baby to enjoy skin sensations, even to like being gently tickled.

This blurred impression is not nearly so marked in relation to the circumoral area of the face. Here is a part of his body with which the newborn is familiar and has had considerable experience. As x-rays show, he may well have found his hands with his mouth and been habitually sucking his thumb or fingers since the twenty-weeks gestation mark. It is reasonable to assume that some exploration of his hands and feet with his mouth preceded thumb sucking. This means that by the time he is born he has been playing with his mouth and hands for nearly half of his intra-uterine life.

Why the newborn spends so much time in oral stimulation is uncertain. It may be a truly instinctive behavior, since it does relate to his survival. While babies born in modern, urban hospitals can be adequately fed whether they are able to suckle or not, the newborn's ability to suckle can still mean the difference between life and death in primitive societies, even in rural ones, where bottles, tubes, formulae, and nipples are not readily available. Small premature babies need to be fed with a tube. But most full-term babies, provided they have been lying in a reasonable position, not too squashed, have been spending hours and days practicing swallowing and are quite proficient.

A breast is always easier for the baby to get food from than a bottle because the food is ejected and the baby has simply to lap it up. He has to suck against pressure to get milk out of a bottle. Either way, however, a full-term baby learns very rapidly how to get his food, once he's been exposed to it and is hungry.

Because he has developed confidence in the use of his mouth, the small baby is apt to derive both comfort and confidence from things taken into the mouth or held close to that part of the face. The habit, shared by so many small children, of wanting something soft close to their faces— a favorite teddy bear or square of blanket which they persist in going to sleep with—derives from the remembrance of the comfort and confidence that it gave them as a newborn to have something that "felt good" in the one part of their anatomy where they could clearly feel. What the newborn holds to his mouth provides him a very real, clear sensation at a time when all other sensation is blurred. A soft blanket tucked around his legs and feet provides no more than a vague, blurred image of warmth, since the baby does not yet know where his legs, feet, or toes are. But he will tightly draw a corner of that same blanket to his face with his hand; he may grasp it close against his mouth, or even suck on it.

The mouth and hands will remain the chief means by

which the baby explores and interprets his environment for many months after he is born. If a small baby is handed a toy, he does not examine it with his eyes as would an older child who is experienced in making judgments through sight. The baby will put the toy into his mouth and explore it with his most experienced tools: his tongue and his lips. As he continues to explore the world around him, he will invariably test the feel of things in his mouth before he looks at them or feels them.

The baby learns a good deal through his mouth. He becomes sensitive to tastes and textures. He will try to put everything into his mouth first so that his tongue and lips can examine the new object and tell him what it is. At this stage he uses his mouth primarily for sucking. Later he will learn to bite and to chew.

Within the first two weeks following birth most babies do not spend very much of their time lying awake. They generally have energy to just sleep and feed. The feeling they experience at this time is not unlike the heavy feeling an adult has in his limbs and whole body when he pulls himself out of the water after a long swim. The baby has been used to even greater weightlessness than a pool or lake provides, and the effort of competing with gravity is at first quite considerable.

From the age of two weeks on, however, the baby begins to have periods when he lies awake and moves about. He is learning to use his limbs. But after a little of this exercise he gets tired of trying to move and he wants something to play with. Since his mouth is the only thing he has to play with at this stage, the baby enjoys something he can suckle on. It's the natural way for the newborn to play.

The lips, mouth, and circumoral area are very impor-

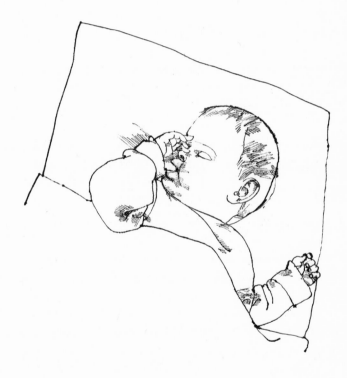

The mouth is often designed to fit a thumb comfortably.

tant to the baby physically and emotionally, and the great comfort that he derives from these first clear sensations should not be denied him. There is every justification to allow the infant to play with a toy in his mouth at this early stage of his development—although the mother should not try to regulate his hunger sensations with it. Nor should the mouth toy be used past early babyhood. The older baby, who has discovered how to play with his hands, his feet, his overall body, his eyes, has plenty else to do; his intellect will not advance as rapidly if he is not given the opportunity to use the new body parts that are now at his command.

Unfortunately, some mothers use the infant's response to oral comfort by keeping something in his mouth constantly in order to keep the baby quiet. This restricts the development of speech and ignores the unhappy child's real needs. Giving an oral toy to a two-year-old is like presenting a teddy bear to a thirteen-year-old. When the newborn has reached the stage where he can sit up by himself, and look around and see things, the mouth toys should be gently but firmly disposed of, not suddenly, but over a period, just as with weaning.

The newborn's other senses are functioning at this early stage, but since he has so little experience with them as yet, his brain does not know how to interpret them. The stimulation to his other senses is confused and unclear. His image of the world, beyond that which his mouth gives him, is very hazy and vague. Consider the persons who have been blind during their childhood years and can suddenly see. When they first see the world, their vision may be good; but what they see is not a meaningful image because the brain has not yet supplied the interpretation of the objects before them. The first vision is always meaningless. Then, slowly, the brain sorts out and identifies objects. Once they have been identified, vision becomes useful and purposeful. Until he reaches this stage, the newborn's visual images are of little use to him. Only through his mouth can he get any clear images.

There is considerable variation in how long the mouth remains the center of the baby's interest and attention. Many babies lose this preoccupation as they learn to experiment with their eyes and hands. Other babies will keep the mouth as the center of gratification and experiment on through the creeping stage; it can become a habit that persists throughout much of childhood. But this extreme is apt to prove true only of children who have inherited a strong tendency to form habits.

Speaking sounds require a completely new use of the parts of the newborn baby's mouth. Before birth, the mouth parts that are involved in sound all had a function, but one that little resembles the ultimate adult use of the mouth. The unborn's lungs are filled with fluid that flows into the baby's throat. The unborn's larynx, instead of being a voice box as in the adult, acts as a sphincter muscle to guard the lungs and prevent hair or skin debris from entering. The unborn's tongue and palate are used to assist swallowing. Only the epiglottic folds in the front of the throat retain their prebirth function throughout life—that of directing swallowed material down the esophagus instead of into the lungs.

The sound that the individual baby makes varies according to the shape of his mouth. The first sounds are created simply by blowing air across the vocal cords. Each baby sounds somewhat different from every other baby because of the size of the mouth, the shape of the throat, and the height and width of the palate.

The small baby hears and knows certain sounds long before he has enough physical control of his speaking apparatus to make those sounds. The speaking sounds that the baby attempts come out at first as squeaks and gurgles which are created well back in the throat. Gradually the voice production comes forward so that he learns to make the "da da da" sounds with his tongue and palate. These sounds are produced in the middle of the mouth. Last of all, he learns to use his lips to make sounds, which include the "mmmm" sounds. This is why babies say "Dada" before "Mama." "Tata," like "Dada," is produced by using the tongue and palate and comes before "Bubub" which, like "Mama," requires the control of the lips. Often small babies make sounds that appear to be recognizable English words—although they are actually only sounds. English-speaking parents get terribly excited when they hear what they think is a word of English from their infant—as I'm sure French parents also do when they think they have caught a word of French.

Babies observe parents or siblings speaking, and it is almost as if they made a mental note that "this is something that's going to prove useful one day!" Small babies often tend to mimic gestures and the motions which they observe accompany speech before they are able to form any words.

The baby who has older siblings has an easier time sorting out words in his mind, since children's speech is very repetitious because of their small vocabulary. These words will soon become familiar to the listening baby, and they will be the first ones that he will attempt to repeat. An only child, who is exposed to adult conversation exclusively, has a harder time learning individual words, since adult speech is far more varied and less repetitive than small children's speech. The only child can be helped to learn to speak earlier if his mother repeats certain words to him, associating them with something that the baby can see, such as his toys and his food.

The baby's attempts at speech are imitative, and he should be talked to by his parents, brothers, sisters, and visitors. "Baby-talk" accomplishes nothing and may even be confusing if the infant gets the idea that communication directed at him must be different from that exchanged between his parents or other children. One should talk normally and naturally to a baby about what one is doing and cares about. If a person is talking just to make noises at him, he will quickly recognize the boredom in the voice and may decide that speech is not a very pleasant pastime after all. It isn't important that the baby understand what is said, but he should find out that people talk and that he, too, will be expected to do it.

When the baby learns to make his first sounds, which are a series of high-pitched squeaks and gurgles from the back of his throat, he will then try this magic over and over again. This form of invention delights him for a while, but when he has mastered it, he gets bored with it and drops it altogether. As he gets a little older he begins to use his tongue and his palate to produce sounds. Now is the time he goes into the "da da da" and "dut dut dut" sounds which so delight his father's ear.

Children vary in their approach to speech, just as they do in everything else. Some will only attempt to repeat a word after they have mastered its meaning and associated it with something they understand. Other children will learn to say sounds, like small parrots, mimicking and repeating them before they have any idea of what they mean. This usually depends upon the kind of memory the child has. An infant who has a good auditory memory will say all manner of words that his ear has "picked up" from adult speech long before he has any clue as to what they mean. Such a child will tend to find phonetics easy and use them extensively in learning to read. Another child may possess a good visual memory. He will learn to read by seeing words and phrases and may become the faster reader. In practice we use both visual and auditory memory, but often are better at one than the other.

Much has been made of the fact that babies can be taught to read, which is quite true. But I would suggest that a baby only learns to read if he very much wants to, and that he should not master reading only to please an ambitious parent. Emphasis on almost any physical or mental feat can produce a child who is ahead of his peers, if he is reasonably intelligent. However, proficiency in one respect may mean that some other useful part of development is either omitted or left behind.

Babies have so very much to learn that it seems a pity to make them specialize at such an early stage. To begin with, they don't approach learning in the same way that school children and adults do, carefully, one step at a time. They are learning everything at once, absorbing from all sides and angles, mastering three or four utterly disparate concepts simultaneously. Teaching them one step at a time may very well slow down their broad range of absorption. Also, it puts a price on accomplishment that may end by producing anxiety—a terrible handicap.

Unless a baby's activities are going to be limited because of disability, it is far more important for him to gain experience and knowledge and proficiency in other ways than reading, which will come in good time. The child will enjoy reading the most who learns it when he wants to learn it. If a baby's physical actions are limited, however, and he is deprived of some of the physical experiences and proficiencies which other children are developing at this age, then I think the quicker he is provided the tool to knowledge that reading represents, the better off he will be. In this case, his eyes must serve as his main gateway to experience and to life.

As the baby gets older and becomes familiar with the use of his eyes and hands and other parts of his body, his mouth may still remain his most trusted tool and chief source of comfort. Especially in moments of confusion or stress, small children are very apt to turn back to their mouths for confidence and succor.

chapter thirteen

FEEDING AND SLEEPING PATTERNS OF THE NEARLY NEW BABY

The newborn baby is too exhausted by his birth to feel hunger distress for several days. Babies vary in the time it takes them to recover from birth trauma. After the baby has slept almost continuously for the first twenty-four, thirty-six, or even forty-eight hours of his extra-uterine life, a strange new restlessness stirs him, wakens him, and makes him cry out. Then, fearful of his own noise, worked up by his own torment, he cries louder and louder. His blood pressure rises with his efforts; his arms and legs wave wildly; he experiences the unfamiliar pangs of hunger distress. He develops a fever in his excitement.

At about the same time the baby's mother feels her breasts grow tense, and now, each time her baby becomes distraught she lifts him in her arms, holds him close, and soothes him, while she feels her nipples tingle and the milk begin to flow. She guides the soft face toward the breast and marvels at the ability of the baby's lips to seek, nudge, and clasp to suckle strongly. The baby suckles three or four minutes at each breast and then settles back into a contented sleep.

On the third and fourth day the baby's distress signals increase to six or seven times within the twenty-four hours. He is quickly satisfied, however, and his mother's milk soon flows freely. From the fifth to the fourteenth day distress signals are heard six times within the twenty-four hours and are quickly answered.

For the first two to two and a half weeks the baby should be given the breast for three to ten minutes on each side, for five to seven times during each day. It is more important to keep a record of the number of feedings a baby has in the day than how much he had at the feed time. By the third week the baby will have worked out his own feeding pattern. Usually this adds up to four or five feedings within each twenty-four hours, at the times that the baby dictates. If he seems to want more than five feedings in a day, perhaps he is not getting enough of mother's milk, in which case a supplemental bottle should be offered to him.

It was once considered sensible to "let baby have a good cry and he will be more hungry for his food." Unfortunately, this works in the reverse, since the tiny baby is apt to swallow a good deal of air when he cries. A baby who is frustrated and angry fills his stomach with air, so that when the feeding finally does come, his stomach signals satisfaction too soon because the air is distending it and making it feel "full." If the baby is not good at releasing this air, he will settle for half a feeding and then wake up sooner and start crying again for the next feed, thus perpetuating the trouble.

Infants vary considerably in the way they feed, how much they want, and when they want it. The times that the baby chooses to feed during the evening hours usually relate to his particular sleep pattern. Humans fall roughly into two distinct types of sleep rhythms, which we call the "owl" and "fowl" types. Some people are definitely one or the other, others not so distinct. This is inherited, like being right- or left-handed, and it differs with different members of each family. (With handedness, too, some people are less distinctly right- or left- —and thus are called ambidextrous.) My youngest child, for instance, is an "owl" like her father, which means that she is very wide awake in the evening, but likes to sleep late in the morning. My second little girl is a distinct "fowl" like me. We rise early and cheerfully, then gradually wear down during the day and want to go to bed early. An "owl" baby will probably develop a schedule of wanting to be fed around ten o'clock at night, and then he will sleep through until five or six in the morning. If he is a "fowl" he will sleep from six at night until around two in the morning and be ready for a feeding then. With many individuals these sleep rhythms are sharply pronounced and with others they are not quite so clear.

At first the baby may not awaken for his feeding at the same time each day, but he will waken for the same number of times in the day. Some babies are extremely dainty feeders and take very small amounts and seem satisfied. These babies, however, tend to awaken more frequently than the usual five or six times in the day. The mother can coax them into taking a little more by encouraging them to rest after they have fed, and then offering them the breast again.

On the other side of the scale, some babies are absolutely ravenous and never seem to get enough. These are often those big, thin, hungry babies who were not able to grow as much as they wished during the final few weeks before birth because of the limitations of the uterus.

They are so hungry and eat so greedily that they may overflow after feeding and are prone to hiccoughs.

One of the many advantages of breast feeding is that the mother can make herself comfortable and even get a little rest while her baby feeds. She can lie down on the bed with the baby beside or on top of her. Milk from the breast is ejected—that is, it runs out under pressure from within the breast—so that even if the baby lies on top of the mother he can feed perfectly well. A woman whose milk is ejected too fast for a baby's stomach to accommodate should lie on her back, with the baby on top, like a little four-legged animal eating. By making the baby suck the milk uphill, both the baby and breasts are forced to work against gravity. In contrast, a bottle must be held in a special upright way, so that the nipple end is always filled with milk—otherwise the baby would suck in air.

The weight of the baby at birth tells very little about his eventual size, since his growth may have been limited while he was in the womb. Immediately following birth there is usually a slight weight loss for the first few days and then the baby begins to gain from a half ounce to one and a half ounces daily. Most babies gain rapidly in both length and weight until they are six to nine months old.

New mothers often worry a good deal about whether the baby is getting enough to eat—especially if he's breast-fed, when they can't see exactly how much he has taken. On the bottle it is easy for the mother to always put in more than she thinks he will take to make sure he is getting enough.

But the only person who knows for sure whether he has enough is the baby himself. Some babies are so lazy that they prefer sleeping to eating. If they feel sleepy at feeding time, they take just a little nibble to last them a very short while and then fall off to sleep, only to waken an hour or so later because they are hungry and want to be fed again. Mothers cannot feed their babies every hour, just because the babies are lazy. If the mother discovers that her baby is doing this, she must make sure that he takes just as much as he will possibly hold at each feeding. If he falls asleep feeding, she can let him doze for five minutes, then wake him up and suckle him again. Usually when she's let him have that little nap, her baby will cooperate and take more food. Some babies never cry for food, possibly because they are not sensitive to hunger distress, just as some women do not feel labor pains.

When the baby slows up a little, the mother should always stop and give him a rest, which will give his stomach time to accommodate the load. If the stomach is filled very quickly it cannot take as much as if it is filled more slowly. When breast feeding, the mother must pause in the middle while she changes the baby from one breast to the other; when bottle feeding, she should put down the bottle and hold the baby for a moment. Holding him against her breast or shoulder will allow wind to escape from the stomach if it wants to.

The practice of burping babies constantly is grossly overdone. A hearty slap on the back does not help bring up wind. Very young babies all have a good deal of air inside their lungs and abdomens because of the structure of their bodies. Newborn babies have a short, wide esophagus, practically no neck as yet, a short chest, and a very long, convex abdomen. There is therefore a "direct pipeline" from the back of the throat to the top of the stomach. They swallow air very readily, and both air and milk come back up easily. You can poke your finger into any infant's tummy and usually raise a belch of air, whether the baby has just been feeding or not. But the air present in the baby's abdomen does not create discomfort. The infant swallows air each time he cries, but bringing up the air is not going to stop his crying. He is most often just hungry.

The only time that "burping the baby" accomplishes a legitimate purpose is when a baby is eating and the mother wants to raise air in the hope of making room for more milk so that he will drink as much as possible and sleep that much longer. But even then, a slap on the back is not necessary. Infants should always be handled very gently. All one needs do to raise air is to hold the baby upright against one's shoulder and gently rub or pat his back. If a mother has a fairly large breast, she can hold him against her body so that her breast pushes gently against his stomach; she will find this a good deal more enjoyable than pounding him on the back.

There is a sort of vomiting, commonly associated with feeding the newborn, which is not really vomiting at all. This phenomenon is medically called "possetting," which infants frequently do immediately after feeding. They simply open their short gullets and spill back all the milk which has not reached the stomach. This is most apt to happen if the baby is laid flat too soon after feeding.

It is unnatural for the clinging type animal to be laid flat on its back all the time. The baby is not only much more comfortable with his head elevated slightly, but he is safer, since flat on his back, he might inhale the milk and choke. The American Indian women had a very good idea for their babies' comfort when they hung them upright on cradle boards. If the mother places the baby in his crib soon after feeding, he should be in a tilted, head-up position. The simplest way to put him on a general slope, so that the upper part of his body will be higher than his stomach, and spilling of the milk less likely to occur, is to prop up his crib. A book placed under each leg at the head-end of the bassinet or crib will give the baby the slope he needs.

While the baby is feeding on the breast or bottle, one should try to protect him from the common cold. Head colds may make adults sniffly and irritable, but they do worse to infants. Bottle babies especially are in trouble since, when their noses are blocked and filled, they need to open their mouths in order to breathe, and they cannot suck properly with their mouths open. It takes a bottle baby suffering a cold twice as long to feed, and sometimes he will give up out of sheer exhaustion before he has had enough. Decongestant nasal drops prescribed by the doctor can be used on the baby a few minutes before his feeding, so that he can suckle without such great effort. Breast-fed babies are somewhat better off since they don't have to work against pressure to get their food. Milk is ejected, so they can clamp their mouths, swallow, and then take a breath.

The biggest help, however, is to prevent his exposure to colds in the first place. This may be almost impossible in a large family, but the mother should be very firm with the other children and relatives and friends, and make it clear that no one with a cold should go near the baby. If a cold made them as miserable, and interfered with their feeding as much as it does with the infant, they wouldn't dream of being so cruel.

Bottle-fed babies are more liable to gastroenteritis infection than breast-fed babies, because of the toxins produced by the bacteria in cow's milk. Human milk also swarms with bacteria, both harmful and harmless, but the commonest and harmless bacteria, lactobacillus, soon lines the intestines of the breast-fed baby like a well-grassed lawn. Because of this, harmful bacteria do not get established in great numbers, just as a scattering of weeds does not take hold on a dense lawn, since the grass stifles them. Harmful bacteria, on the other hand, are apt to grow in cow's milk, even in a refrigerator, since a frosted-up refrigerator may be as warm as room temperature in its middle shelves.

Another bacterial infection that is common to babies is due to the peculiar pubertal state of the baby's skin. Like the adolescent's skin, large numbers of harmful bacteria can accumulate in the active sebaceous glands of the baby's skin. These glands are highly active in babyhood, to the extent that some appear as raised red spots which the mother may call "heat spots." Outflow of sebum may be hampered. Practically all skin infection starts in blocked glands or pores. Harmful bacteria are so freely distributed on the human body that they are always awaiting a chance to multiply and cause damage, and whenever a gland is blocked the secretion provides the right environment of warmth and moisture to feed the bacteria. Boils, pustules, furuncles, impetigo, acne—all have their basis in a blocked gland. It is important to keep the baby's skin clean, and as far as possible, to prevent secretions from accumulating. But one should not attempt to sterilize the baby's skin by too vigorous germicides. A bath once a day with warm water and hexachlorophane soap is sufficient, plus, of course, sponging areas which need it during the day. The baby needs some bacterial cover on the skin, just as he needs it inside his intestines, to build up immunity to infections.

Babies' teeth appear according to the individual pattern of development. The first tooth may show up when the baby is five months old, or it may not come in until he has reached a full year. Occasionally a baby is born with a front tooth. Since the infant will get twenty milk teeth within his first eighteen months, "teething" has for years been a catch-all to describe any fretful behavior. Some babies do show a definite irritability for some time before each tooth appears, while others surprise their mothers with a tooth one day with no advance warning. Babies all dribble when their teeth are beginning to come in, and their biting-chewing urge increases tenfold, so that soon nothing within their grasp is safe from being chewed on.

Infants' fretfulness and irritability is often attributed to teething when the cause is actually something else that is common to the same period. There is a disease with almost identical symptoms—infection of the middle ear (otitis media). The infant suffering from this will be feverish and fretful, and will not feed well. Since teething is considered to produce these symptoms but by no means always does, the possibility of ear infection should not be overlooked. Sometimes the baby is helpful in diagnosing this ailment by frequently putting his hand to one or both of his ears.

Babies can start learning about solid food, as an auxiliary to their milk diet, at six to eight weeks of age. A mother shouldn't be startled by the grimaces the baby may make the first time he is approached with some strange-looking spoonful of food. He has every reason to be apprehensive. And if he does taste it, and finds he does not like what he tastes, she may just as well put that food aside, to try at another time. The very young baby can be fed a variety of flavors—vegetables, egg, bacon—

and if he's hungry he will eat it. Later, as his sense of smell becomes more acute, he is far more selective about what he will accept. Vegetables especially may offend him, and he may violently reject the peas or cabbage he happily accepted a few weeks before. For now he can smell them and he wants no part of them. As his taste develops, he is much more sensitive to strong tastes than adults are. He is not being bad tempered and un-co-operative when he violently rejects certain foods. The infant's taste is so fresh and keen that disagreeable flavors can actually be painful to him.

Children have a wide range of taste. As the baby grows older, his appreciation of taste, as well as of colors and shapes and sounds, grows keener. The main thing to realize is that children have tastes quite different from those of adults. Most adult taste has been dulled by smoking or drinking or just by strong foods or hot drinks, and it takes something sharp to excite the adult palate. The child, however, has fresh taste buds and a very strong appreciation of flavors. Some children derive all the emotional satisfaction they want from foods with the very simplest tastes, while other children of the same age like something stronger. In my own family the oldest and youngest child will try, and usually enjoy, almost any flavor of cheese or shellfish, for example; the middle three are far more conservative and won't touch such foods.

No one diet will be suitable for every child, either in tastes or quantity. Each individual has his own rate of growth and food requirement. The baby's utilization of food is inherited. If the parents both use up the food they eat and neither one has a weight problem, then the child will probably be the same. If, on the other hand, there is a tendency to fat, the parents should look ahead to the development of their child and not encourage him to habitually stuff himself. Even while the child is still an infant, they shouldn't stuff things in his mouth to keep him quiet. For if a child has an inherited tendency to be fat, it will be very difficult for him to later learn to control the bad habit of stuffing himself.

The idea that children should be taught to "clean their plates" of everything served to them is ridiculous. An adult cannot possibly determine how much the child wants. Children up to the age of seven usually leave some food on their plates. But the parents should not worry about what the child does not eat. Each child has his own growth rate and his own food requirements. Given a fair range of choice, he will take the food he needs.

Before the days of penicillin, the only means we had to treat childhood complaints was with bed rest and diet, but now neither treatment has much meaning. When the mother of a sick child asks me what she should give him to eat and how long she should make him stay in bed, I tell her I really don't care. If the child feels sick enough he will voluntarily go to bed. But if he wants to run and play, then he should be allowed to do so. My husband always points out, "More people die in bed than anywhere else."

Modern mothers need not worry about special foods for a sick child. Given any reasonable choice, the sick child, as well as the healthy child, will select a diet adequate for his current needs. In the old days sick children and adults were always put on special diets of beef tea and soft custard and rum butter and the like; while these are good, it is now unnecessary to make a fetish of illness.

Babies also vary a good deal in their behavior during the course of the day. Some babies are absolutely uproarious at night, while others are exhilarated and lively in the early morning. Newborn babies are often conditioned to activity at certain hours of the day from their unborn state, such as their penchant for being carried around at the hour their mother was always bustling around getting dinner.

The baby's energy is also sometimes related to the output of fat in the mother's milk, which will range from a peak of nine percent fat content down to as low as one percent within the course of each day. The lowest point, or trough, for the mother occurs in mid-afternoon. The baby who chooses to feed at this time is very likely to cry for more food within two hours, since he doesn't feel as though he has eaten anything. This is because the fat content of food "tells you you've been fed" and gives the baby a full, satisfied feeling which lasts. After two or three months a breast-fed baby will sleep better at night if given at suppertime a custard made from one egg yolk (white may cause allergy), one cup of milk, and one teaspoon sugar heated together in a double boiler until thickened. It can be fed from a teaspoon when cooled.

Parents often create unnecessary headaches for themselves by trying to train or discipline their infants into feeding and sleeping patterns that would be most convenient for the household. Unfortunately, the baby's feeding and sleeping patterns are inherent, and in some babies are very strong. If a mother wants to keep peace with her baby, she should learn his rhythms and adjust accordingly.

Infants simply do not take kindly to any efforts at discipline. They are much more keen on letting their wants be known and tended to than they are on trying to please their parents. They neither understand nor appear to tolerate parental efforts at training. I have never seen infant discipline create anything except a distressed baby.

The baby whose waking periods are inconvenient for his parents can usually be encouraged to go back to sleep if the mother changes his position or gives him something to cling to with his hands. But to isolate or ignore him or leave him to cry will not improve his sleeping pattern.

The amount of sleep each baby requires also varies a great deal. After the first two or three months, all babies will spend much more of their time awake. Often they continue to wake up at night after the night feeding has been discontinued. A contented baby may wake up, stay awake for a while, making noises and playing with his hands to amuse himself, and then drift back to sleep again, without disturbing his parents. If he wakes up and needs changing or feels lonesome, however, they will hear about it.

Until he is six months old the baby does not need a pillow because his head is as wide as his shoulders and there is no gap which needs to be filled in when he is lying on his side. When the baby is lying on his back, the back of his head—which was born first—is quite moulded and developed, like a Hottentot's, so that a pillow would push the head up into an uncomfortable position. When the baby is lying face down, a pillow would interfere with his breathing.

After the baby is six months old, however, and he has begun to develop an indentation between his head and back, he can use a small pillow that is firm enough so that he won't be able to bury his face in it. Parents worry unduly about the possibility of suffocation. A normal, healthy baby does not suffocate. When deaths attributed to suffocation are investigated, they usually turn out to be cases of respiratory infection rather than suffocation. The time that parents should be concerned about whether the baby is getting enough air is when they have him in an automobile. They should never leave the baby in a car unless the windows are open.

Small babies should be put in their cribs facing a different way following each feeding. If they are always left to lie on the same side, they may develop a flattening of the skull (which is still soft) on that side. While this is not a permanent defect, it will not disappear until the baby sits up for the greater part of each day.

The sleep needs of the infant lessen as he gets older. From sleeping for nearly twenty-two hours out of each twenty-four, which he does when he is first born, the baby, by the end of his first year, will probably need only two naps each day, one in the morning and one in the afternoon, in addition to his night's sleep.

Some babies experience difficulty both in getting to sleep and in staying asleep in the evening, during their first three months. They regularly become distressed each night and cry, and picking them up and holding them does not help them settle down. Such babies suffer a painful abdominal distress known as "three months colic." They experience periodic attacks of pain in the lower bowel, thought to be due to the presence of excessive air. Since the gas or air is not manufactured in the intestinal tract, this air has been swallowed some ten to twelve hours earlier. Relief comes when the air is passed on downwards. Sometimes putting the baby on his tummy or giving him a baby aspirin tablet dissolved in water helps. The most heartening thing about this condition is that the baby will outgrow it, and infants seldom have it past the age of three months.

When a baby does finally fall asleep it is not necessary

for the mother to keep the whole house quiet. Infants do not need absolute silence to stay asleep. Both adults and babies are wakened not by noise, but by an unequal level of noise. This is why adults and children can sleep on moving trains and buses, yet will wake with a start when they stop at a station. If the radio is playing when the baby is sleeping, and then someone snaps it off, the baby will probably wake up, since it is the sustained intensity of sound that kept the baby sleeping.

chapter fourteen

THE NEWBORN BABY'S BOWEL AND BLADDER LEARN THEIR FUNCTIONS

There is considerable confusion and misinformation, even among those professionally involved in infant care, about the bowel and kidney functions of the newborn baby. While much attention has been devoted to the psychological aspects of bowel function and toilet training, I think it is important for parents to understand first something about the physiology of the human excretory system.

Prior to birth, neither the fetal kidney nor the fetal bowel function in the adult sense. The fetal bowel does accumulate a certain amount of waste and cell debris during the intra-uterine stage, but it does not empty until after the baby is born. For the first two days following birth, this accumulation appears periodically as a blackish, tarry substance known as meconium. This is not the same as the dietary waste that the bowel will later excrete.

At birth, the baby has in his stomach a combination of swallowed air and blood. He may vomit mucus which appears to have "coffee grounds" in it, dark brown specks which are blood particles. The baby may also pass bloody-looking movements; this does not mean that he is bleeding internally, but only that he swallowed some blood during birth.

When yellowish motions are established (after two or three days), they may often have a greenish cast which worries mothers. The coloration that would be considered abnormal for an adult, however, is not abnormal for the young baby. The green pigment is caused by the early function of the liver and the bile from the gall bladder and is not a symptom of any disorder.

As the newborn starts feeding, and the bowel begins to excrete actual dietary waste, the pattern for elimination is extremely variable from one baby to another. This variance is also physiological. The movements for at least the first two months of the baby's extra-uterine existence may be either very frequent, or very infrequent. In neither extreme, however, should the newborn ever be "dosed," and no mechanical efforts should be made to regulate his excretory system before it has had a chance to get its own machinery in good running order, and settle into its own individual pattern. Green fluid, bubbly motions are dangerous, and the mother should call the doctor, taking care to keep a sample diaper.

When the food reaches the stomach of the newborn baby, waves of muscular action in the stomach wall first cause the food to be well mixed with gastric juices. Then, like a mechanical loading machine, the waves force the contents of the stomach—which now consist of partially digested food—on down into the narrow duodenum, that portion of the intestinal tract which lies just beyond the stomach proper.

The same type of muscular waves next move the food, which is now gradually being absorbed or converted into waste material, on downward into the lower bowel. It is only when the waste reaches this point in its journey through the body that the baby, or the adult, has any awareness or sensation about the whole process. When the waste reaches the lower bowel, it can be felt as a "load," a heaviness near the anus. Before that, the peristaltic action of the intestines, the digestion and assimilation, all occurred at a subconscious level.

There are two reflex actions involved in this process which differ in different babies. First, there is the gastro-enteric reflex. This refers to the continuous waves of peristaltic action which occur, throughout the voyage of the food, all the way from the stomach, where it first appears as undigested food, clear down to the rectum, where it arrives as waste material. In some babies this gastroenteric reflex is so strong that there is a direct ratio between what he eats and the action of the bowel. The moment the baby's stomach is filled, the lower bowel empties whatever waste is accumulated there—like a busy hostess in a small house who lets people out the back door when she hears new arrivals at the front. The mother of the newborn baby that has this sort of simple gastro-colic ratio will have a dirty diaper to contend with after each feeding. The waste that the baby eliminates is not from the food he has just eaten, nor even from the feeding immediately prior to that, but from what he ate twelve hours before. It's very simple to demonstrate this fact by merely feeding the baby a little chocolate syrup! It will be eliminated around twelve hours later.

Other babies evacuate much less frequently than this. And at the opposite pole from the baby whose bowel mechanism is triggered by every feeding is the baby whose body does not set up a reflex for elimination until it is totally full, which takes eight days. This great range in the excretory mechanism of the small baby is why "normal" elimination may be anything from eight times a day to once in every eight days.

It is very wrong to dose the newborn baby for either constipation or diarrhea, although this is sometimes advised by people who really should know better. Very rarely does a young baby have any bowel disorder that would justify medication, though lubrication with bland paraffin oil is sometimes indicated if the movement is very hard. And if the baby does have some disorder, it is impossible to properly diagnose the condition until the baby's bowel has settled down and worked out its own pattern.

Eventually, as each baby's body becomes accustomed to the regular intake of food and production of waste, the reflex action settles into a pattern similar to the types we find in older children and adults. There are three medical "norms" for the excretory system: an evacuation once a day, twice a day, or once in two days. The infant will achieve one of these three patterns at around two months of age.

The second reflex involved in the baby's excretory system is the "feeling" he experiences when the bowel is full, which gives him the conscious desire to evacuate. At first the newborn baby empties his bowel without knowing why he does it. Later, he comes to associate the feeling of the full bowel with the emptying effort, and he will consciously apply the required effort. The infant derives great emotional pleasure from the outcome of this conscious effort.

A mother soon learns to tell when her baby is getting ready for evacuation. But even after she is able to anticipate this, it is probably not advisable to use a potty seat

until the baby is big enough and strong enough to sit comfortably, so that he will be happy sitting up for ten or fifteen minutes. Even then, putting the baby on the potty
accomplishes little in the way of training unless the proc-
cess is repeated daily. This cannot be done without developing undesirable tensions unless the baby evacuates at
approximately the same time each day.

The important thing about early training is first of all,
that the mother should wait to make any attempt at using
a seat until the baby is able to sit easily and comfortably.
Secondly, she should wait until the baby shows a regular
pattern of evacuating, which any healthy baby will soon
do if he is getting sufficient fluids and a reasonably even
food intake. The time to start training will be anywhere
from nine months on, depending on the rate of growth
and the excretory pattern of the individual baby.

Teaching the baby can be started quite early, without
too much discipline, provided the baby enjoys what he is
learning. The purpose of starting early toilet training
should not be simply that it saves washing, but that it will
facilitate full training—which is achieved with the control of urination.

Happily, the baby really enjoys the sensation of bowel
evacuation. If the mother takes advantage of this natural
predisposition to learning, she can easily and pleasurably
(and from the psychological standpoint, a-traumatically)
teach her baby to use, and to enjoy using, the potty.

A second natural aid to toilet training is the fact that
the baby does not like to be dirty or to lie in a dirty mess.
Even the newborn cries to be changed so that he can be
clean and dry again. When changing the diaper of the
small baby, a mother should be especially careful not to
frighten him. The experience of becoming clean again

should always be a pleasant one. She should be careful not to prick him with a pin, which would make him wary of the next change. If she finds that he has a raw, sore bottom, which may happen to any little baby under six months of age, she should leave the diaper off for a while so that his buttocks may be exposed to the air to dry and heal. In the first few months, the baby passes urine so frequently that it is impossible not to have him lying in a wet diaper once in a while. Fortunately, as he gets older his tender skin toughens and he urinates when awake or partly awake, and not during deep sleep.

Psychologists are quite right in paying so much attention to this period of development, since the way in which this learning is achieved can certainly have a marked influence on the individual's later attitudes and personal happiness. Psychologists warn parents not to make a fuss if the child is wet or dirties himself, lest the feelings of guilt and self-deprecation incurred by this attitude harm these normal functions of the body where there is a delicate balance between willed action and autonomic function. Those functions most readily upset by anxiety (which disturbs the balance) are elimination, digestion, and sex. Toilet training should be handled in as simple, natural, and matter-of-fact way as possible, with no good-evil, right-wrong aspects to it. An exaggerated emphasis on "being clean" can affect a child's personality, and contribute to his becoming overly-conscientious, overly-cautious, and overly-strict, both in his demands upon himself and others.

But the argument that all efforts at toilet training the baby be delayed because of possible bad psychological effects also overlooks some other important aspects of infant behavior. A child likes to do things that his parents do; he likes to mimic and, most important of all, he likes to be comfortable. If the baby is having a regular bowel action daily by the age of ten to twelve months, what is more comfortable for him than to sit on a little seat with his toys around him for a few minutes? No praise or blame need enter the picture. It does not take the baby long to realize, after he has tried it once or twice, that sitting on a little seat for a while is far preferable, from the standpoint of sheer comfort, than having a gooey lump in his pants and having his bottom scrubbed.

Toilet training is one means by which the small child's phenomenal capacity to learn can be utilized to excellent advantage. While the small child's willingness to learn should not be exploited, as it is when adults force infants to specialize, such as the Russians do with their three-year-old acrobats and the Viennese with their infant opera singers, I think it is fine to let the baby learn something that will be a happy step forward for himself and his mother.

The small child shows very early that he enjoys "accomplishing" something, and he enjoys pleasing his mother. These two traits can be used to advantage in toilet training, provided the process is presented as a pleasure rather than a discipline.

To provide a proper setting for training, the mother should purchase a really comfortable, steady potty seat where the child will feel relaxed and secure. The baby actively dislikes both isolation and darkness, so the mother should not shut him up in a dark bathroom, to sit out his fifteen minutes alone. He will not enjoy this, and he may react by withholding the elimination. Also, the baby's sense of smell is daily becoming more acute, and he will not enjoy being confined in a close, smelly room.

The potty seat should by no means be a part of his high chair or have any association with eating. The chair that I found best suited my own children was rather oversized by most manufacturers' standards, and very comfortable. In the warm weather, I carried it outside and set it on the back porch in the sunlight, where the baby could sit and enjoy the fresh air. The baby was not isolated, since I was within sight and call.

I began teaching my babies at from six to ten months of age, depending on the baby. All five responded very well to this maneuver and were happy on the potty for bowel evacuation by the time they could walk, at from one year to fifteen months of age. This method might not get the same results with every child, but it's worth a try. If the baby is trained to like the potty and associates it with a pleasurable act, this will lead on naturally and easily to later training for urination.

The baby's bowel regularity is very easily upset by colds, cutting teeth, illness, or lack of fluid. If he is happy about co-operating when he can, then his inability to perform is most likely due to some functional upset, *very often the first sign a parent has.*

The control of the bladder takes longer for the infant to master than bowel control, simply because the kidney before birth served quite a different function. Within the womb, the fetal kidney develops along with the unborn's other organs, but it does not function in the adult regulatory sense. The kidney produces copious dilute fluid which passes into the baby's bladder, is temporarily stored there, and then passes on into the amniotic sac. The kidney does not get rid of the baby's body wastes. Those wastes —of which there are actually very little since most of the baby's food has been pre-digested before he gets it—pass along the umbilical cord to the placenta, and then into the mother's blood stream, where they are eventually excreted through the mother's kidneys and lungs.

After the baby is born, the kidney very slowly turns into an efficient excretory organ. At first it is so patently inefficient that the only way it is able to rid the baby's body of waste is by pouring out great quantities of water along with the waste. So long as the kidney operates in this profligate fashion, the newborn needs a relatively far greater amount of water than does the adult, whose kidney can efficiently produce a highly concentrated urine.

Thus, it is vital that the young baby should have plenty of fluid. His kidney cannot concentrate urine efficiently and cannot function at all without floods of water to rid his body of the small amount of waste. If the baby's fluid intake is curtailed, his bowel first shows the lack of essential fluid by producing dry movements or none at all, and the baby becomes severely constipated as the bowel attempts to conserve what water it can. Since the kidney functions only with the aid of large amounts of water, the baby loses his body fluid with his urine and thereby becomes dehydrated. Severe illness and even death can come quickly to the newborn who is deprived of water.

To be well and stay well, the newborn baby must drink large amounts of fluids, and must pass urine abundantly and frequently. This is why it is almost impossible to do any training of the small baby in regard to urination. If the mother tried to catch all this kidney function in a potty, she would have to be on the job all the time. Before the days when diapers and diaper services were plentifully available, the baby's prodigious kidney action was sometimes handled by laying the newborn on a little grid, so the fluid would drip through, just as a roast might be put on a grill to let the fat run off.

Still another factor, besides the frequency and amount, makes urination training more difficult and complex than bowel training. The newborn baby empties his bladder whenever it becomes full. To learn to "hold on" for another moment, which is necessary when using a potty, the baby has to understand what his mother expects of him. And he has to want to please her enough to learn to do what she wants.

Fortunately for mothers, children are born mimics. They like to do what their parents do, and they show a strong desire to please when they are still a good deal under one year of age. This desire to please varies with the individual child, according both to his inherited temperament and to how much encouragement he gets from his parents. The child who knows that he is being noticed and approved of will learn fairly quickly what his mother means when she suggests that he try to hold on for a minute, until she has time to fetch the potty.

The technique that I evolved for urination training has been not to attempt to teach the baby anything—other than to let him know that I know when he is wet—until he walks. When he has gotten to be nine or ten months old and I notice that he is wet, I'll say, "Oh, let's get dry" or something to that effect, so that he knows that being dry is preferable to feeling wet. Then when the child has learned to walk, or is well up on all fours, I dispense with diapers except for sleep times. Small, easily removed pants are substituted for the diaper during the daytime hours.

The daily pattern for training is based on a simple physiological principle: blood dilution reaches its maximum within one half to three quarters of an hour after a drink, and this stimulates kidney action. While not cutting down on the baby's fluid intake, after he is walking I give him three large drinks of milk a day, not a lot of little ones as adults tend to have; I put him on the potty a half hour after each drink. If the big drink is given just before a rest period, then a mother can wait and potty the baby as soon as he wakes up. If she gives him a lot of small drinks, she will have more problems.

This routine is actually not much trouble once it has become established, which usually takes about one week. In the morning, when the mother first picks up the baby, if he is dry she can take him to the bathroom with her. Mother and child can use the bathroom together conveniently at this time, which will help prove to the baby that this is something that mother does, too, and it will encourage him to imitate her.

Then the baby gets his first big drink of the day, in a bottle if he prefers it that way. Breakfast is served to all the family. After that it is time to put the baby on the potty to catch his first big morning drink.

The second big drink is given the baby before his morning nap, and he is taken to the potty when he awakens. After lunch the baby can be left until his bath, unless he seems irritable, which may indicate he is uncomfortable and perhaps needs to urinate again. Otherwise he can be left until it is time for his bath, when he is bound to urinate in the bath water. The third big drink is given at bedtime.

This daily schedule adds up to only about four or five times on the potty during the day, and each time it only takes a matter of minutes to slip down the little pants and put the baby on the seat.

As is true of bowel action, the baby's urination may be affected by such things as colds, cutting teeth, or illness. Although it may sometimes seem that he is not really progressing in his training at all, the mother must not be upset by any shift in the baby's performance. Above all, she should not worry her baby about it. Nothing will set him back further in his training than the idea that he is not pleasing her. All human beings need encouragement. With babies and with small children it is vital to their development.

chapter fifteen

GROWTH PATTERNS OF THE INDIVIDUAL INFANT

Growth is not a mere linear progression, as many believe it to be. The growth pattern is actually a series of "fits and starts," with alternating periods of lengthening and rounding, from conception through full maturity. The little three-month fetus is in a rounding stage of development. Then, from the third to the seventh month of his intra-uterine life, the unborn baby goes through a rapid period of elongation, during which he grows faster in length than he will again in his lifetime. Within those four short months, the unborn baby grows from twelve to fourteen inches in length. Then, in the seventh month, the unborn baby goes into another rounding stage; this lasts through his birth and on until he reaches six or nine months of age.

Because of this established pattern for growth, it is normal for all six-month-old newborn babies to be chubby. They are as fat then as they should ever be. As if in anticipation, the newborn baby has loose folds of skin all ready to receive fatty deposits. If the baby does not go through a fat stage at from six months to one year of age, he probably will never be fat throughout his childhood, although he may still become a large adult.

There is no reason to worry about the tubby six-month-old or year-old baby, or to cut down on his food for fear he will become too fat. This is his time to be fat, and he will lengthen out, with little increase in weight, as he goes into his second year. One mother I knew so wanted a delicate-looking child that she starved her new baby and made him an anxious, wailing fellow. The baby went right on developing a big skeleton, however, since that was his inheritance, and as soon as he reached the age (of nine months or so) where he was able to insist he began making up the weight that corresponded with his bone structure. He was certainly never a chubby baby, but his sturdy shape at two belied all his mother's attempts to make an elf out of him.

Around one year after birth, the baby goes into another period of fast lengthening that lasts about a year. It is of this age that old grannies used to say "the baby is running off his fat." It may have appeared that way, but it was only coincidence that his lengthening growth occurred at about the same time that he started to crawl around and walk. The baby does not actually lose weight during this period. His weight is merely rearranged on his lengthening body.

During the first-year rounding stage the baby usually gains from fourteen to eighteen pounds over his birth weight, so that the average seven-pound baby will weigh from twenty-one to twenty-five pounds at one year of age. But during the second year, as he adds height, he puts on no more than two or three more pounds. By the third year, when he moves into another rounding phase, he adds from six to eight pounds of weight. The child will, of course, grow in height all the time, but the rate at which height is gained is phasic and interspersed with periods of increased weight gain.

When height growth is steadying off, weight may catch up somewhat so that the preschool child looks cherubic. Grade-school children exhibit slow and steady growth in both height and weight. There is an interesting parallel between the rapid elongation in the unborn baby and the preadolescent growth spurt. Between the end of the third month and late pregnancy the fetus grows as much as four inches in a month. In the preadolescent spurt the boy or girl may shoot up four inches in a year. At both times there is an increasing level of sex hormones in the blood and both spurts are followed by a rounding off and the enlargement of sex organs, a tendency to a rash on the face and so on.

While children certainly should not be starved, they also should not be stuffed. If the child has inherited a genetic tendency toward fat, his parents are doing him a great disservice if they add to his inheritance by encouraging the habit of overeating. They are not being kind to the plump child when they urge him to clean his plate, or tempt him with extra helpings. The six- to ten-year-old who is plump when he should be growing leggy and lean can look forward to a weight problem the rest of his life—which only the strongest will power will ever control. Not only does appetite become a habit, but bone structure gradually increases to carry the load.

Fortunately, the six- to ten-year level, when a genetic tendency to fat becomes noticeable, is correspondingly the time for the beginning of self-discipline. While one cannot ask for self-control from a toddler, one can start teaching a nine-year-old the sort of behavior and self-control that will shape him for social life ahead. If the child is fat, parents should try to win his co-operation in reducing his food intake. And they should try to protect him from grannies or aunts or friendly neighbors who buy his affections with cookies and cakes. Some early firmness and judgment can save this child from a lifelong problem.

The final rounding stage for girls occurs between the ages of twelve and sixteen when they go through their adolescent "puppy fat" period. The alteration in the distribution of adolescent body fat relates to sexual development. Girls, with breasts enlarging and subcutaneous fat increasing, round out both face and figure, and skeletal changes emphasize hips. This sort of chubbiness and roundness is natural and acceptable in the adolescent, but it should not be allowed to run on into the girl's wedding day. If a girl's adolescent plumpness has not begun to thin out by the time she reaches sixteen, she should be encouraged to diet and learn to control her weight. Boys are less liable to "puppy fat" but exhibit marked muscular development and are about two years behind girls in showing adolescent changes.

In skeletal as well as all other growth and development, girls mature ahead of boys. Their gestation period in the womb is shorter than that of boys by from two to three days. In their skeletal maturity, there is an average of three years difference, so that girls stop growing in height from two to six years earlier than boys do. Long bones cease to grow and anatomical development ceases and is consolidated around eighteen for girls, and twenty-one for boys.

While the amount of body fat waxes and wanes with growth, the body members exhibit their own differential growth rates, which causes the child to have less appealing contours at some stages than at others. From classical times beauty and grace in the adult have been synonymous with a head, neck, and trunk approximately as long as the legs, while the head approximates one seventh of the total height. The physical bulk of a baby's head is, at birth, greater than any other designated part of his body —bigger than his abdomen, or chest, or even both of his legs. In fact it makes up one quarter of his total length. Nor is the head proportioned as it is in the adult, for the cranium, housing the brain, is huge in proportion to the lower face. At birth the weight of the brain represents eleven percent of the baby's total weight, while in adults it is no more than two percent. The lower jaw, at birth, is so little developed that the chin appears to recede, though the eyeballs and much of the internal ear are nearly adult size. The cherubic nose, turned up so that one looks straight into the nostrils, will alter years later when the nose bone begins to grow. With his soft, maneuverable little nose and recessive chin, the baby has a face well suited for suckling, which he does with his toothless upper jaw and his powerful tongue. The upper jaw is ahead of the lower in its development through much of childhood, and it is not until adolescence that the lower jaw finally catches up. This partly accounts for the child's "buck-toothed" appearance around ten or eleven, although the size of the permanent teeth may contribute. In some children the upper jaw and teeth are literally so large in proportion to the rest of the lower face that the lips cannot conveniently close over them. The open mouth at ten is a feature of differential growth rates and has nothing to do with adenoids, which ordinarily recede at about seven years of age. Because the temples are the most protuberant part of the face, in the nursery they carry the bruises, though the front teeth and nose will come in for their share at grade school.

We are seemingly escaping well out of babyhood in our consideration of growth, and for a good reason. Growth, whether in height, weight or of the body members, is what the visitors or the visited comment on, and, upon his growth, all too often, the child is judged. The parents, seeing the child every day, will not be greatly aware of change in size and shape after the first months, but every time granny or aunt calls, attention is immediately drawn to how the child is growing physically. It is as well to be prepared, not only for how the baby may look when he is born, but for his future development too. There are certain times in our lives when physical attributes have a greater appeal than at others. The newborn period is conventionally not a period of great beauty. The skull is big, often hairless or too hairy, and looks misshapen. Those same eyes which will have sufficient appeal to draw out every camera at six months look too big and heavy-lidded at birth. Fathers may be a little aghast at the lack of chin in newborn sons, not suspecting perhaps that the lower jaw grows more slowly than any other part of the head.

Books of baby photographs are full of appealing chubbies aged six months or more, not of preemies or even full-term newborns. Only the hands and feet of a newborn seem to have a general appeal. However to those privileged to attend a birth there is nothing more beautiful than the wet, wriggling, pink, protesting womb-escapee.

The differential growth that occurs in the spine accounts for some of the aesthetically pleasing or displeasing postures that children adopt. A baby lying on his tummy and holding up his head to look around makes a pleasing pic-

The short thoracic and long abdominal spine
produces this posture necessary for balance. The
legs too are wide apart, whether or not he
wears a diaper.

ture. At the time that he learns to do this his spine is fairly straight, except in the neck, where it is fast developing a forward curvature. By the time the baby can sit up unsupported another curve has developed, this time in the chest region. This second curve is backward, thereby balancing the neck curve. As yet the spine below the chest is fairly straight, so that the mechanics of the sitting baby are forward curve in cervical (neck) spine, backward curve in the dorsal (chest) spine, straight lumbar (abdominal) and pelvic spine balanced by legs as props out in front.

To advance from the sitting posture to the standing, and be able to balance while standing, the baby needs to develop a forward curve in his lumbar spine and a compensatory backward tilt in the pelvis. The age and rate at which this is achieved vary. It is by no means necessary that a creeping stage should intervene between the sitting and the standing achievements, and many babies prefer to move about in the sitting posture or to wriggle along on their tummies rather than creep. In terms of development, early man's forest-reared baby probably did not creep but proceeded to haul himself up from the sitting posture, and when he was sufficiently stable, to cast off and walk.

The erect posture is achieved by a series of compensating curves in the spine, and because of differential growth rates the small child cannot comfortably attain the adult ideal of a flat abdomen and straight legs. Not only the head but also the abdomen is relatively large in babyhood, requiring a rapacious food intake. On the other hand, the pelvis and buttocks are relatively small. All young children need to stand with their tummies poking out (before the standing age, even the navel will often protrude) and in compensation the pelvic tilt will cause the knees to turn in. Knock-knees go along with the toe scramble, and to avoid this the child keeps his legs apart. The protuberant tummy may not offend the adult, but the apparently misshapen legs may, and a mother may trot her four-year-old along to the doctor to find out what is wrong with his knees. Posture disparities of this kind sort themselves out as the legs and chest lengthen. As the child grows the abdomen hardly changes and the same pair of short pants will fit for years. Not so the shirts and long pants. In days when clothing was more expensive, it is hardly surprising that mothers dressed their boys in knickerbockers instead of long pants. While the knock-kneed appearance should have entirely disappeared by the age of nine, the persistently fat child may never outgrow it and usually compensates by walking with his toes turned out for life.

In fairy tales, good and bad fairies presided at the birth with their various gifts. However, we receive our gifts long before birth as part of our inheritance. Much of posture is inherited, and there is an ideal posture for each body type. Fashion does not always favor a particular type: the girl with the long abdominal spine and rather hollow chest who can achieve the languid, willowy look may triumph today, while a shorter, rounder shape may be "in" tomorrow. Fitness faddists and fashion leaders should not try to arbitrate posture for everyone.

As the baby grows many of the things about his appearance may offend the current adult sense of beauty, but these are temporary and should not cause alarm.

chapter sixteen

WHAT IS HEREDITARY
IN THE NEWBORN

The basic blueprint for the baby's appearance, inside and out, and for his general body function was contained in his original cell at the time of conception. A child is born a certain type of individual, and no parent, nor anyone else, will be able to alter the basic blueprint. If parents have given birth to a potential painter when they hoped for a priest, there is nothing for it but to give the child the maximum opportunity to develop what he is, provided it meets with standards acceptable in our society. We are fortunate that modern society offers such a wide variety of opportunities for skill, and that the dexterous child may triumph as a Houdini rather than as an illegal safebreaker; the supreme sailor can receive Federal pay and not have to rely on buccaneering as in Drake's day.

Let the bird have his flight, the cheetah his speed, the deer his grace; man's greatest asset is his brain. Most people have probably seen a famous tapestry, or mosaic, or handwoven carpet and marvelled at the intricacy of the design and the mastermind who contrived it. The first plan would have been laid out graphically, with markings to indicate where the colors or pieces would finally go. Then, with infinite patience and skill, the artist would set about to stitch or set or weave the masterpiece. The brain in the beginning is just such an unworked but marked-out design. This design is not completed by the time of birth, though the impatient artist already has started to fill in some of the squares. Years—perhaps eight or more—must pass before the full complement of working units are added to the human brain. But the artist does not wait. He goes on with the detail of color and blend and unity of his masterpiece just as well as his environment will allow.

Each of us is the craftsman who stitches or sets or weaves his own brainpower on a canvas that already carries a design. We start before birth and we can go on improving our brainpower almost indefinitely.

The fundamental design of our brain, its potential, comes through heredity, from the generations before us. Our environment, the studio or workroom in which we spend the time creating our mind, is very important in the initial years when new components are still being added to the brain. As with the tapestry, a serious defect in the environment in the early years may cause a tear in the canvas or a knot in the thread which could take half a lifetime of patient work to eradicate. Or a strain thrown across the canvas may warp the whole design. To call the brain a tapestry is a vast oversimplification, for it is a million times more complex, yet the lesson of the warp or the knot remains.

One's brain is unique. There has never been another exactly like it in the long history of mankind. Obviously one cannot know how a baby's brain will function or what parts of its overall function are superior in terms of what he will need to find a suitable niche in contemporary society. Some basic trends do become apparent quite early to the alert parent and can be used in providing the appropriate "do-and-learn" type of plaything popular now. For instance, a child might inherit a very good picture memory. He may notice differences in clothes, show recognition of places he has been to before, like things to be put in the same place so that he can find them immediately. A child with this inherent ability, when learning to read, will prefer to learn whole words at a time and will resort to phonetics very little. Another child might have a rather poor picture memory and depend much more on auditory memory, that is, remembering the pattern of sound. Such a child can be taught to speak early, has no difficulty in mastering phonetics, and uses them intelligently to spell words that have no meaning for him. Having "an ear for music" is not simply an inborn trait, though there are those who have considerably more trouble in distinguishing pitch and tone than others. Some children are fascinated by color, others by pattern, still others by problem and solution. One little boy I know makes a problem out of everything. When asked to bring in four eggs from a nest containing five, so as to leave one for the hen, his immediate reaction was, "I wonder which one the hen would like to keep."

All our learning, and consequently all of our subsequent voluntary ability, depends first on sensations coming into the brain. The level (or amount of stimulus) at which the brain receives a sensation varies from one person to another, and, in the same person, from one sensation to another. Thus there is the child who is rather unresponsive to pain and yet highly responsive to sound; the one whose muscle and joint sensation is so sensitive as to enable him to be way ahead of his peers in physical prowess, yet for whom shape and pattern have little meaning. Taste and smell, appreciation of touch and temperature, appreciation of emotional atmosphere, and all the other senses—each of them, like pain, can be appreciated to a degree that is almost crippling right through to being never felt at all. Children born insensitive to pain crop up occasionally, rarities thankfully, and gaily break their arms and legs and noses with never a murmur. Color blind, tone deaf, heartless or clumsy children exist, but there is rarely one who, born wanting in one sense, cannot be helped and encouraged to use his other senses to make up the deficiency.

The environment in which the growing brain accepts sensory stimulation and reacts to it is very important. At one time it was believed that babies thrived best if kept in a dark, quiet place on the ground, such as that which nature provided for them in the womb. We know now that this is by no means always true of the womb or of the baby. Parents should find out just what their baby does find most reassuring. Is he a type who likes warmth, quiet, and subdued light, or is he nervous and upset when he finds himself alone? It is a great mistake to start with a preconceived notion of what the baby will like. Too much solitude can be damaging. A dozen years ago, as part of my training, I worked in a small country hospital which had only three wards—one for males, one for females, and one for tubercular cases. There was one surgeon and one physician, and both were omnipotent. The surgeon had among his male patients a baby boy who had lain from birth on his back, for months and months, with his feet in plaster. He had had the misfortune to have big feet that had not fitted neatly in the womb and had twisted inward, potentially club feet. Rather than turn him over to his mother's loving neglect, the surgeon had decided to make certain that the feet grew properly. How the child's brain got along with nearly a year staring at the same blank ceiling is anybody's guess.

Although we invariably refer to the baby as "he" in the text, we use this generically to indicate a member of the genus "man," and not to indicate preference or superiority. In terms of sheer durability girls are born significantly superior. In terms of intelligence there is probably no difference between the sexes. A woman who has excelled in a man's world (and there is no reason for this to be a goal, as women already have sufficient challenges on their own plate) generally comes from a family predominantly of girls with a very capable and interested father. Presumably, had there been sons, the father would have concentrated his training upon them instead.

Temperament, which roughly speaking means cruising speed, is also inherited. It may or may not be a case of "like parent like child" and can lead to a lot of exasperation. The terms temperament, intelligence, and personality are invented to denote certain human traits that are not separate or independent entities. In isolation, any one of them is as useless as a heart without blood or a liver without glycogen. They are of some significance as filing compartments for statisticians working in millions, but applied by individual parents to individual children, they are misleading and dangerous. Like "normality" in childbirth, diagnoses of temperament, intelligence, and personality are best made in retrospect. When a child is grown up, his parents are entitled to say that he is intelligent if he has done well at school and college (though the reverse is not true), that he has a good personality if he makes friends easily and is approachable, and that his temperament is alert or docile. Psychologists and educators, discovering the inadequacy of these terms, are avoiding them. Parents are unwise to put children in these artificial categories and should concentrate on providing every opportunity for them to develop their abilities.

The likely inheritance of the adopted child is not as much of a "blind guess" as one might suspect. There is apt to be a marked similarity of genetic pattern in a baby that is adopted from the same racial background as the parents. Each of us has two parents, four grandparents, eight great-grandparents, sixteen great-great-grandparents, and so on, so that to go twenty or more generations back involves millions of ancestors. Since this number exceeds the population of, say, the British Isles at that time, two people who derive from British stock must have some common ancestors. In the same sense all people of a given racial group have some common ancestors within the period of genetic influence.

While the baby's temperament and appearance are inherited, the conscious learning process will affect personality. For the newborn so much in the outside world is a new experience. He has very limited previous association into which he can fit the fresh facts. While the adult mind has a mass of pre-established information and association, so that when anything new crops up it can easily be related to other knowledge, the newborn first must acquire knowledge of all he experiences.

Fortunately, the baby is impervious to failure. If failure meant to the newborn and to the infant what it so often does to the adult—embarrassment, guilt, self-deprecation—the baby would be far less willing to expose himself to failure, and his rate of learning would be far slower.

But since the baby happily has not yet associated failure with its emotional context, he goes right on making mistakes until he has acquired the knowledge he desires. When a baby is trying to walk and falls down, he only cries if the fall hurts him, not because he fears he has made a spectacle of himself.

The potential rate of learning of the individual does not alter during his lifetime. What does alter is his willingness to accept failure. The apparently slower rate of learning of the adult is actually not so much a slowing of any mental processes as a fear of ridicule. One of the reasons that small children are so much more skilled at picking up foreign languages than adults is because they attack it differently. While the adult proceeds slowly, trying to master one step at a time, the small child simply opens his eager ears and eyes and learns all he can at once. He soon effortlessly absorbs enough of this new language to be able to communicate in it, while the adult is still laboring to perfect a verb. When the baby first decides that he wants to learn to talk, he does not master a single word at a time before moving on to another one. He tries all the words he can imitate, practices them all, and masters them all.

The baby and small child's learning is triggered by the most natural and powerful of impulses: a desire to discover the world around him. He is not learning things in order to please his parents or his teacher, but only to satisfy himself. His curiosity leads him, and he attacks learning in a rapid, reckless, all-embracing fashion, absorbing a million disparate things at the same time, untroubled by logical steps or the fear of making an error. Only later, when he discovers that mistakes are considered misdemeanors and are punishable, does he consciously slow down and tailor his rapid rate of learning.

Since so much of the initial embroidery of the child's pattern of personality and learning occur in the first half dozen or so years of his life, it is during this period—from birth to the age of six or eight—that he should be provided unlimited opportunities for exploration and experience. An educator said recently that we could best help our children if we thought of ourselves as gardeners rather than teachers. The gardener does not grow the flowers; he provides the most suitable situation for the flowers to grow themselves.

Parents who worry that the child's breakneck curiosity may lead him into pitfalls should consider that there is no such thing as a completely un-traumatic upbringing. To begin with, there is parental fallibility at times. But there is also the child himself, who is already a strong individual with desires that, in their very nature, demand disappointment. It is only natural, during infancy as during later life, that frustrations will alternate with gratifications.

Since the child must learn by experiment, parents should try to avoid saying "no" and "don't" to many things. If the child's need for discovery provides an inconvenience to the parents, this fact of parenthood should be accepted with grace. Habitual "no's" restrict a child's learning. On the other hand, his environment should by no means be all sweetness and light. A little turmoil has no harmful affect on a baby's development. The normal chaos, and clash of activities and personalities in a busy household is an infinitely more interesting atmosphere for the baby than an artificially peaceful milieu. The placid, subdued household is not adequate preparation for the turmoil he will eventually face in the outside world. Worse, it is a dreadful bore. Children are very easily bored, a fact which any parent who has watched his infant examine a new toy for a moment and then toss it out of his crib knows all too well. When the baby throws the toy away, he is saying that he has already discovered everything interesting about that particular plaything, and he is now ready for something else. Studies have shown that the baby of one year can find out all he wants to know about the average toy in ninety seconds.

The parent can be of most help by providing the knowledge-thirsty baby with the maximum opportunity for physical exploration and for communication with others. The less physical restriction the small baby has, the quicker he will get on with his discoveries about the world.

Most of the baby equipment that we have today was designed to please parents rather than babies. The average baby carriage accomplishes two very unpleasant things so far as the newborn baby is concerned: it keeps him in an unnaturally and uncomfortably flat position, and it keeps him at arms' length from his mother at the period when he most enjoys being close to her. He can't even see her very well as she trundles him down the sidewalk. He is isolated in his wicker-framed world, with only strangers to stare at, and no one to touch. His mother might as well have paid an attendant to wheel him around, for all the good her presence does her baby.

In New Zealand there was a period when young mothers bought dreadful, oversized English perambulators (nanny-type) which glutted the sidewalks and made life hazardous for pedestrians. Mothers dolled up their babies in frilled and starched dresses, propped them in one of those enormous carriages and strolled through the streets, sometimes, alas, two abreast. The babies could not possibly have been comfortable with all those clothes on and so thoroughly isolated, so I assume the object was to show off the mother and the coach. I trust the custom now prevalent in America, of using those very lightweight wood or plastic cradleboards (infant seats) will spread to our country. They take up very little space, and keep the baby very near his mother, where he can see her. The mother can also keep the baby in the center of the household activity by moving him around in one of the seats; while not actually holding him in her arms, she can keep him near her and the other children while she tends her household chores.

One practical use I see for baby carriages is inside the house when the baby is sick. Then a carriage can be quite useful, like a rolling bed, which the mother can draw up close beside her own bed, when she wants to be near enough to the baby at night.

My dislike for huge carriages is mild compared with my hatred of the so-called playpen. The playpen symbolizes the entire concept of penning and restricting small babies as though they were bad dogs. If used constantly, I am convinced that the playpen could succeed in keeping the baby from ever learning anything. I never owned a playpen nor any contraption that resembled one.

The only possible advantage of a playpen is that the mother can know precisely where her baby is. If she cannot let the baby loose in the house to crawl about as he chooses, she can let him have one entire room in which to make his voyages of discovery, and fence off the door only. She can take out whatever things she feels might be dangerous, and then let him go free. Whether the floor is carpeted or left bare really does not matter. The baby may slide a bit more on the bare floor, but it doesn't hurt him, and he can develop his grasping control with his toes. If there is any tendency toward allergies in the family, the baby should be kept off carpets, since they collect quite enough house dust to endanger an allergic child.

The only way the baby can learn is by trial and error. This is the basis of all learning for all ages. Parents should not put up barriers to their child's learning. It is all well and good for the mother to fulfill her role by keeping her baby clean and dry and warm. But there is more to motherhood than that. Such physical comforts are only a part of what the baby needs. Parents cannot stand in the way of his learning about himself and the world around him, even if his mistakes and misjudgments are an agony to behold. One or two tumbles—physical or mental—are essential to mastering any new thing. I let my children crawl around the house wherever they decided they wanted to go, although I most certainly kept my eye on them. A mother can no more leave an infant unattended than she can a soufflé. I recall one mother who was obviously shocked to see that I let my "crawlers" edge their way down a short flight of stairs. Of course they took some tumbles—all children do. But they go down more carefully next time. Of course if someone is agitatedly wringing his hands beside the baby, some of the tense atmosphere will brush off on him.

The development of physical dexterity in the infant is partly hereditary and partly the result of repeated practice. While most infants appear to use their entire hands in a clasping reflex, little Japanese babies play with very complicated, small, ingenious toys, and learn delicate manipulation of their fingers while they are still very young, through constant practice.

One old wives' tale which crops up in all cultures is that

babies become bowlegged because they have been allowed to walk when they were too young. The baby dictates when he is ready to walk, and he walks when he feels like doing it—which varies in age with different babies. Bowlegs are the result, not of walking too early, but of the baby's not having been given a proper opportunity to bear weight on his legs before he began to walk.

If a mother holds a six-month-old baby under his arms she will notice that he stretches his legs out, like a swimmer, exercising them by letting them take a share of his body weight. When she holds the baby on her lap, he will try to pull himself upright so that he can test his legs for standing. While it is still impossible for him to stand unsupported, he can take his body weight on his legs if he is helped. All healthy babies want to stand up in someone's lap. It's often a considerable nuisance—especially to the women in the family—since it makes their skirts so untidy, but the baby is very strong-willed about his desire, and will insist on standing. He needs to exercise his legs, and build up their strength so that they will be in good shape when he begins to walk. He should be allowed every opportunity to do this.

The human body is like a bridge. If the stresses on the bones develop in the right way, perfect posture will be achieved. If the baby does not practice standing up—supported by an adult—and take weight on his legs before he commences to walk, the stress lines in the bones will not develop properly. Then, when he tries to take all his weight on his underdeveloped legs, they will bow out under stress. This condition is especially true of the child who is congenitally heavy and fat.

Another area of the baby's development where parental patience can prove very helpful is in his efforts at communication. The infant, as we have pointed out, is aware of speech at a very early age, long before he can imitate the sounds himself. His brain absorbs the oceans of sounds that wash around him, and he eventually sorts out individual ones and attempts them himself. As soon as he tries to make words, the baby should be greatly encouraged in his desire to communicate. The baby's older brothers and sisters can be of considerable help, since "teaching the baby" by repeating words until he catches onto them makes a very good game for young children.

Such efforts are more demanding for busy parents, but they should by no means be neglected. The parents whose conversation with their children is limited to "yes" and "no" are crippling their communication. In a recent study of school dropouts in the first five grades in the public schools in New York City, it was reported that a basic fault shared by all of these children was not, as had been suspected, anatomical defects; it was simply a failure in their ability to communicate. The children did not understand the speech of others well, nor could they speak well themselves. The child who found it impossible to communicate with his teachers was the child who had not learned to communicate with his parents within the home.

Taking one's place in society, and learning how to live with others, requires, in addition to knowledge, self-discipline. Discipline is meaningless to the infant. Only certain limited disciplines can be learned by the three- to seven-year-old child. But starting at eight, the child can be made aware of an ideal and be encouraged to attain it. It is possible to start helping him to undertake the self-disciplines which will make things easier for him as an adult. The eight-year-old is amenable to the development of such good habits as weight control, improvement of posture, attention to manners, and the development of good work habits.

If the child can learn such useful social patterns at eight and nine, they will provide him safeguards during his teens. It is as a teenager that the child first learns to live independently, spend his own money, get around by himself. If he already knows how to handle himself, then he will face his teens unencumbered by the urge for rebellion. He will appreciate life, and in valuing his own privilege to be alive will not abuse his privilege to give life. If, on the other hand, his parents have persisted in doing all the disciplining themselves without giving the child a chance to learn how to deal with himself, then, when he reaches his teens, he will react to this overdiscipline by trying to prove his independence in antisocial ways.

The knowledge, and the self-knowledge, that the parents have allowed and encouraged the child to develop will provide the tools for his adult life. A very great part of this equipment was gained for us during our formative, infant years.

chapter seventeen

A NEW UNDERSTANDING
OF THE INFANT YEARS

*What Fetology Will Mean to the Unborn
and Newborn of the Future*

Until the turn of the century, infant death, disease, and malformation were simply accepted as the "will of God" by both the medical profession and the lay public. Three out of every ten children were destined to die before they reached one year of age. In our own mothers' childhood, such diseases as rheumatic fever, pneumonia, and tuberculosis commonly took a heavy toll of child life and health. Since then, however, advances in medical care of children have lowered the infant death rate, so that today the child of one month to one year of age has as good a chance of attaining maturity as children from one year to adolescence.

An attitude of resigned fatalism still persists, nonetheless, regarding miscarriages, very premature babies, and stillbirths. Especially with stillbirths the resignation tends to border on complacency, since the actual percentage of stillborn infants is relatively low. It should be remembered as an incentive to further work in this field, that stillbirths are not spread democratically throughout any community, but tend to recur frequently among a few people, so that the same parents often bear a disproportionate burden.

So far as death and disease in the unborn child, medicine now has passed from a period of resignation to one of recognition that these things, just as in adults, are caused by adverse factors which can be studied—and eventually circumvented.

The commonest, and very often the only, check that the doctor makes of his unborn patient is to listen to the fetal heartbeat to find out if the baby is alive or dead; this indicates how crude our procedures for diagnosing the unborn patient actually are. Our ignorance of fetal maladies would be appalling if it applied to adult medicine. We are only recently, through the new branch of medicine known as fetology, beginning to probe the mysteries and the needs of our unseen patients. Since our ignorance is so great, most of the work being carried on in fetology today is still in the research stage. Much of it is being done with animals and still needs to be applied to the human baby. Fortunately for the unborn of the future, we are at long last tapping this vast unknown reservoir of medical information.

Such current concern for individual fetal life might seem somewhat ill-directed, in view of our world population problems and the growing necessity for family restriction. Humanity, in this past century, proved itself capable of producing its own kind in quantity. Now, we must give more attention to the quality of our offspring. In our search for quality, however, such barbaric practices as those of the late Nazi regime, which purported to be aimed at improving human quality, cannot be tolerated. There is no human quality without love, since love is essential to human dignity. It forms the basis of our ability to communicate (establish rapport with others), which first placed man on the ladder enabling him to climb the tree of development higher and faster than other animals. In learning to love, and then to communicate with his young and with his fellows; to store and use knowledge communicated to him; to add to it from experience and apply it to altered circumstances, man developed a brain. He is not governed much by instinct. Even such fundamental behavior as mating and caring for young is not instinctive to man. Chimpanzees reared artificially from birth out of sight of others of their kind have no idea how to mate; if artificially impregnated, the female will in time bear a baby which she completely neglects because she does not know instinctively to put it to her breast.

If all babies were wanted, we would have no population problems. It is the unwanted, the illegitimate, the unfed that have made population control necessary. In a recent policy statement the American Medical Association envisages that "the prescription of child-spacing measures should be available to all patients who require them, consistent with their creed and mores." "Birth control" is in itself an unfortunate misnomer. It implies infanticide, such as the Chinese once practiced when they destroyed their girl babies. Correctly we should speak of "conception control," since this term adequately describes all the methods acceptable in the English-speaking world for limiting our population to those babies who will be properly cared for.

If our worldwide efforts at population control were based on conception—rather than birth—control, I feel our position would be better understood by other cultures. For this would at least imply that we are sincere in our claim to value human life. In the prevention of conception by mechanical, physiological (rhythm), or pharmacological means, no life is done away with. Nor are couples cruelly denied their marital rights. Men and women need one another; they need a physical union which has continuity. Conception control allows them to make a clear decision about how many children they want and feel that they can adequately provide for.

To conceive a child is the greatest privilege most of us will ever know. It is the one occasion in a couple's life as parents when their decision is paramount. They can decide that they wish to conceive a child, but that is where their absolute decision ends. Their baby's genetic constitution, gestation, birth, youthful growth, and maturity can only be assisted, never directed. For one brief moment, parents hold the power of creation, the power of insuring a little earthly immortality for themselves.

There are some who believe that mankind's power to give life should be extended to allow him to then take that life, provided it has not reached a given maturity. In most courts of law in the English-speaking world the unborn is without rights. Killing him is not called murder, or even the lesser crime of manslaughter. In cases trying abortionists, the baby is never mentioned. Apparently only the mother's life and welfare is at stake. Yet all of us, if we count for something now, also counted for something before we were born. Until individual fetal life is regarded as valuable, will people stop to think twice about shouldering the great responsibility of bringing new life, wanted or unwanted, into the world?

When should one have a child? Other things being equal, a baby's life should be begun when the parents are deeply in love with each other. This applies not only to the first baby; all babies should be conceived in love, and nurtured in love through the various crises that occur before, during, and after birth. Because human fertility is very variable and no couple knows how readily they will conceive until they have tried, this must be considered an ideal rather than a necessity.

It is important both for the parents and their baby that conception take place at a time in the mother's life when she can adapt successfully to her pregnancy. The mother should, optimally, be sexually well adjusted at the time of conception. Both time and experience are required before the normal woman is successfully adapted to sexual life and finds it emotionally satisfying. Adaptation in all things does not follow a smooth, straight line. Rather, it involves a marked (hyper) reaction, followed by a steadily maintained reaction (a hillock of reaction which drops off to a sustained plateau). At first, both partners in sexual union experience many simultaneous sensations—pain, tension, lust, fear, trepidation, excitement—so much sensation, in fact, that it can hardly be received by either one with completely ecstatic enjoyment. However, if this pair is suited to one another, their mental, emotional, and physical reactions will adapt and reach a harmonious plateau, which, far from proving dull and uninteresting, will work out to be ultimately more satisfying. If, on the other hand, they fail to adapt, both partners are left distraught and unsettled.

Women can be thrown into a state of turmoil which makes adaptation to sex difficult if they conceive a baby during the hillock phase of their sexual adaptation. To add morning sickness, qualms about pregnancy, and possibly hasty arrangements for a wedding and perhaps facing irate parents, to the adaptation to sexual life, can prevent a harmonious plateau from ever forming. It is, therefore, better for a woman not to conceive during a honeymoon, or before, if she is really considering the welfare of her marriage and her baby.

When both partners have adapted to a harmonious plateau in their sexual life, they will usually feel a strong and urgent desire for complete fulfillment of their actions in the creation of new life. Parents should remember that the decision to withhold all barriers to conception is the only decision that nature permits them to make in the birth of their child.

If she is planning a pregnancy, the mother should aim for optimum physical and emotional health in the months before she conceives. We now have reason to believe that it is probably of even greater importance for the woman to follow a good diet and keep check on her food intake before she conceives than it is during her pregnancy, after her baby has become master of the table. During their late teens, many women experience irregular menstrual periods, which are often the result of vitamin deficiencies. Were conception to take place at this time, the uterine environment would not be the most favorable for the fertilized ovum to flourish.

Fortunately, in our culture, males place a high regard on their mate's ability as a cook. A husband is not likely to countenance a diet of hamburgers and Coke. It is probable that the bride, regardless of the limitations of her diet as either a teenager or a busy career girl, will learn to set a good table and serve a balanced diet of meats, vegetables and fruits, to please her husband.

So far as the baby's nutrition is concerned, four distinct stages can now be recognized. In the first stage, which lasts but a day or two following conception, the dividing cell depends on nutritional material that was already stored in the ovum; the ovum, you will recall, greatly exceeds the sperm in size because of this store of nutrient material. In the second stage, when the immature embryo consists of many dividing cells, called the blastocyst, it floats freely along the fallopian tube into the uterine cavity. This sac of cells is growing fast, and it derives its nourishment from the fluid secretions in the tube and the uterus. Medicine is still in a state of profound ignorance so far as precisely what nutrients are required at this stage of life; but that these nutrients—whatever they are—are of critical importance to the new life is evidenced both by the high incidence of early miscarriage and by the proven effects of drugs (taken by the mother) upon the embryo at this time.

The third stage is the early implantation, when the fetus has burrowed into the lining wall of the uterus, but has not yet established its own system of circulating blood. At this point, nutriments must reach the rapidly growing and developing fetal tissues by diffusion—absorption from the surrounding uterus—which once again calls upon the nutriments that the mother's body has already stored and ready to offer.

In the final, true placental stage of fetal life, which lasts throughout the major part of the pregnancy, the fetus not only has an organ (the placenta) for sorting and storing his food, but he also has his own beating heart and system of blood vessels with blood to transport the nutriments and oxygen to all parts of his growing body. At this stage the fetus has become a complete parasite, and he dominates his mother's body. Now her diet is not of such critical importance as it was at the beginning stages of his development, before he had his own machinery in good working order.

In late pregnancy, the size of the baby is not strictly related to his mother's nutrition, unless she has been eating far too much. Thus a doctor cannot use size, even as determined by X-ray, to accurately determine the baby's age. Although bone ossification does give a rough guide, the most useful pointer to the baby's due date is the date of conception or else the date of the last normal menstrual period.

In assessing fetal health, the doctor now watches the changes in maternal function very carefully, for he has learned that it is actually the mother who is a passive carrier, while the fetus is very largely in charge of the pregnancy. The way in which he lies in the womb, and the way in which he presents himself at birth, both appear to be the result of his active and purposeful search for a position of comfort. The maintenance of the pregnancy is also largely determined by the fetus and his placenta, which, through an intimately interwoven biochemical reaction, manage to produce the hormones which are necessary to sustain the pregnancy for both mother and child. And he plays an active, rather than inert, role in the birth process. Birth for "the passive passenger" used to be considered a hydraulic process, in which the baby was forced out, under pressure, like a cork from a bottle. Because of this theory, almost the only fetal factor considered important was the diameter of the fetal skull. Any obstetrical problem that could not be solved mechanically, by pushing, pulling, or cutting, was destined to remain unsolved. Now we have discovered, through an understanding of the "splinting" process during uterine contractions, which does not force the baby's head downward, but straightens out his entire body, changing him from a rag doll into a tin soldier, that the hydraulic theory is entirely wrong. The baby is not an inert champagne cork popped out under pressure, but an active voyager navigating a long and tortuous course into a strange new world. Mechanical assistance answers only a percentage of his possible needs.

Another medical fallacy that modern obstetrics discards is the idea that the pregnant woman can be treated as a patient alone. No problem in fetal health or disease can any longer be considered in isolation. At minimum, two people are involved, the mother and her child.

Thus blood tests, once considered to be necessary only as a check on maternal health, now test for the presence of some antibodies in the maternal blood which would pass the placenta and adversely affect the fetus. It is well known that most antibodies in the maternal blood do go through to the fetus to some extent, and that most are useful and protect the baby from infectious disease in the few months following birth. Those antibodies which are not useful, but in fact very damaging to the fetus, are the so-called Rh antibodies. These may develop where a mother with Rh negative blood carries a child whose blood is Rh positive. On the grounds that around fifteen percent of Caucasian women have Rh negative blood, it might be assumed that one pregnancy in eight would be affected by Rh antibodies, while in fact only one pregnancy in two hundred is found, when tested, to be complicated by them. Both the mother's ability to form these harmful antibodies and the permeability of the placenta to them are thus variable. We do not know whether the placenta is also variably permeable to other antibodies.

Only one pregnancy in two hundred is affected by hemolytic (Rh) disease (that is, one in two hundred of *all* pregnancies, not merely those where the mother is Rh negative). These pregnancies require careful checking for the effects of the antibodies on the child; if tests on the amniotic fluid indicate the need, the baby may have to be delivered before term. Ninety out of every hundred hemolytic disease babies can be managed this way, while ten in a hundred tests will indicate that the baby requires a blood transfusion before birth in order to be born alive. In a city of two million people of Caucasian stock, between twenty and thirty babies a year would require this more extensive medical care.

Toxemia is another condition which the modern doctor views in a new light. This condition, which shows as an overloading of the mother's body with fluid during pregnancy, has, until very recently, always been treated as a maternal disorder. The doctor suspects toxemia if the woman starts to gain excessive weight in the final three months of her pregnancy. The mother herself notices it when her feet and ankles swell. Toxemia, however, is not a disease in itself, but a symptom, an outward sign of a condition of the pregnancy. But what is it a sign of? It may, just as a headache, indicate a number of different underlying conditions. Headache can be caused by anything from head injury to an overdose of a drug, and may even result from a condition outside the skull, such as sinusitis. The causes of toxemia may be equally diverse, ranging from the mother's dietary condition to fetal causes, to metabolic or cardiovascular conditions. With headache, a woman may very well dash to a drugstore for aspirin, without bothering to ascertain the cause. A doctor can ease the symptom of toxemia by prescribing tablets which will reduce the fluid content and make his patient more comfortable. But he cannot merely write a prescription without first endeavoring to ascertain the cause. Recently the effects of toxemia on the baby have been measured by an analysis of the end products of the baby's hormones which are present in the mother's urine. The effects upon the baby of the conditions producing toxemia are almost invariably greater than the effects upon the mother. Through further research, we may derive clues to the management of this disorder, which will result in the best care for both patients.

Some of the most tantalizing questions about pregnancy still remain unanswered. What precise conditions start and maintain labor? How can it be stopped?

We know that control of labor is much more of a fetal than a maternal function, but precisely how, when, and why it begins remain incompletely answered. There is strong evidence that the pituitary gland in the baby is at least partly responsible for initiating the process of labor. When the health of the baby depends on not waiting for the natural onset of birth, labor can be started—and maintained—synthetically by using an intravenous oxytocic drip, with which the hormone oxytocin is dripped into a vein at such a dose and rate as to set up strong, regular contractions. Somewhere between fifty and two hundred contractions are required for full dilation of the cervix. For accuracy a mechanical recording device is used to measure the activity of the uterus. The process is time-consuming, expensive, and if not performed by conscientious, well-trained hands, it can be dangerous.

But while doctors have found means to induce labor, and carry it through synthetically, we as yet know of nothing that will reliably stop a contracting uterus once it has gone into labor. True, many women will swear that something they were given or something that they did stopped their labor contractions, but nothing that has been claimed has proved really effective. Very often a woman thinks that her labor has stopped if the pain of the contractions is blotted out with drugs, but a hand on the abdomen will register that effective contractions are continuing.

Treatment of the unborn is made very difficult because once the uterus is opened (as it has been in the experiments with fetal surgery) labor will start up in a few days or weeks, and nothing can be done to stop it. Sometimes, after an intra-uterine transfusion through the intact walls of the uterus, premature labor will start. Our saddest case was an unborn baby who underwent three very successful transfusions, but a few days following the third one, the uterine muscle discharged him from the womb. He was born fit and well, living entirely on "borrowed blood," only to die the following day from prematurity, which is one of our greatest killers. So much more could be done in the operative line and the prevention of prematurity if only we had the ability to stop labor.

The adequacy of the care we can offer the prematurely born baby is still incomplete. One of the major problems is nutriment which can satisfactorily substitute for the pre-digested piped-in food supply of the womb. Much of this work is being carried out through a study of marsupials, since these animals, such as the kangaroos and the opossums, give birth to their young while they are still immature, then carry them about in their pouches until they are fully developed. One doctor working at an animal research station in New Zealand is currently investigating the secretion that the marsupials have available for their young. From this study we may learn how to create satisfactory alternatives to cow's milk to feed premature babies.

Another killer and crippler of infants is anoxemia, a condition in which the fetal oxygen supply is, for some reason, diminished; this has been blamed for everything from undersized babies to malformations, and is now the subject of intensive investigation. By taking samples of the fetal fluid during labor when the cervix has dilated, and later, when the waters have broken, by sampling a drop of blood from the baby's scalp, German doctors claim that anoxemia can be detected before birth. In these cases, the baby can be delivered by mechanical means before permanent damage occurs. From these tests we should eventually get a much clearer picture of the real risks of anoxemia during labor and delivery. And if anoxemia is indeed the villain it has been thought to be, the more serious effects may be averted by routinely inducing deliveries whenever this condition is detected.

Other mechanical methods of diagnosing the unborn that are already in use are machines which can chart the unborn's heartbeat (electrocardiogram) and chart his brain waves (electroencephalogram). We inject dyes into the amniotic fluid that he drinks, so that we are able to x-ray his organs as well as his skeleton. Ultrasonic devices provide pictures of fetal body tissue, and are also being used to detect abnormalities. And there is another alternate to x-ray, the technique of thermography, which pictures the fetus by means of the heat which radiates from the mother's body.

In our treatment of the unborn as an individual patient, one of our major lacks is any form of fetal medication. Research in fetal pharmacology thus far has identified a list of drugs (taken by the mother) which might damage the unborn. But we know almost nothing about what sort of medicines might help him. Adult medicine, however, was once at this same stage, so we can hopefully look to a not too far distant time when we will have learned fetal medication, so that we can treat our unborn patients as effectively as we do the newborn.

The effect of drugs used successfully in adults must be carefully assessed in children. It is not safe to merely reduce the dose. This principle applies to an even greater extent to the fetus. The fetus, for one thing, has a much more complex physique and metabolism than his mature counterpart. At birth he leaves behind much that was an intimate part of his anatomy before. So much of his metabolism is frankly so different in the unborn state that we are only on the brink of understanding it. The mother is producing growth hormone, particularly if she is young and still growing herself. Will that make her baby grow? Will he get too big for her? No. The baby is growing at a tremendous pace, but not under the stimulus of the pituitary growth hormone which operates in the child. There is so much evidence of the differences in his metabolism, so much for research to discover. One fetal tissue which fascinates researchers in many fields is the trophoblast. This outer cell layer of the very young embryo enables the embryo to dig into the spongy lining of the uterus. Trophoblast cells destroy uterine cells, using them as nourishment, and advance like a cancer. The uterus somehow protects itself from too great incursions of the trophoblast cells. Exactly how it does this is a mystery, because no other part of the body can do it. A trophoblast implanted anywhere else in the body will eat away whatever tissue it comes in contact with. It was recently discovered that the trophoblast would even eat away cancer cells—a finding of extreme interest to cancer researchers.

Not only parents, doctors, and research workers but also

anthropologists, sociologists, and psychologists should look more closely at the fetus.

By studying intensively the newborn, his behavior, his reactions, his body function, his whole being, and then relating this knowledge to what we already know and what we suspect of him before his birth, and what we know and suspect of early man, we can learn what we most need for the future.

Immediately prior to birth, we find the human baby living in a warm, moist environment, markedly similar to the humid, tropical regions of man's beginnings. He is both structurally and functionally fitted to live in the conditions in which early man existed, as a hunter in a hot, wet climate. A hairless creature, early man was capable of dissipating excess body heat through sweating, and thus could outrun and outmaneuver the animals upon whom he preyed.

The human baby is born for just such a life. Given plenty of fluid, his bodily defenses against overheating are very good, although his body can cool many degrees before his defenses to cold are alerted. At birth, the human infant has five hundred to six hundred sweat glands per square centimeter, in contrast to his parents, who have adapted to a cooler climate, and therefore have only one hundred to two hundred per square centimeter. Even in cool climates, the newborn has four times more water put through each kilogram of body tissue than the adult does.

Once early man moved away from equatorial regions into cooler climates, he had to wear protection against cold, and his body metabolism had to increase to keep him warm. This meant increase in muscle tone, blood pressure, pulse rate, and food requirements. In colonizing the cooler regions of the globe, he learned to make use of clothing and of fire.

Man's tremendous power to adapt to environments for which he was not fitted has recently been demonstrated by a Russian couple with four children. Raising them on a Spartan regime which includes sleeping all winter on a porch with a window open and only a sheet for covering, and wearing nothing more than shorts the year round, the parents have shown that the children can adapt successfully to the cold. Yet the children's bodies show a rise in metabolism so great that their growth rate has been slowed down and their blood pressures are well above normal. It is interesting to note that the Russian pediatric authorities do not approve this experiment. Yet, we have found that a moderate degree of cooling can raise human efficiency. Physical prowess is improved and the tempo of work is increased in cooler zones. As an example, on the purely physical level, there is a twenty-five percent reduction in the rate of running one mile in the tropics of Australia, compared with the same mile race performed in a temperate zone.

There seems to be no evidence that evolutionary changes in man have in any way modified the conditions in the womb. Certainly, as man has evolved, the genetic inheritances of the baby have shown great differences in shape, color, etc. But the function of the placenta, the amniotic fluid, and the umbilical cord; the gestation period; the mechanism of expulsion, all seem to be largely unchanged. If this were not so, different racial groups would exhibit differences in pregnancies, just as they do exhibit differences in size, color, and feature.

From the apparently eternal form of human pregnancy we can deduce that the first children born to early man over a million years ago had precisely the same *in utero* experience as children born today. However, the *ex utero* environment has altered. Protohominid's (proman's) child was born into an environment so similar to the one that he had just left that he did not need clothing, diapers, playpens, toilet training, spoon feeding, cribs, or any of the other paraphernalia we associate with infant care today. In a warm climate his metabolism would work at its most efficient level, and milk, even watery milk, so long as it was abundant, was all he would require for effective growth until he had several teeth. There would be no bottom rashes or routines or formulas and very little crying. Carried most of the time, the baby's ability to cling would improve rather than diminish, and from this would come the ability to haul the body up against gravity; once balanced in the upright posture, he could cast off and walk without first creeping (a method we still occasionally see in some babies today).

This shows that many of the problems we have with our babies have been created by ourselves. The faster we expect babies to adjust to a strange environment for which they were not prepared at birth, and to become miniature adults, the greater our problems are. It is certainly pointless to attempt to impose adult standards even earlier and earlier, as some "authorities" would urge us to do.

Our greater understanding of the fetus can help too in the education of children. A small child cannot be expected to relish the advent of a new baby in his household, but he can be helped to regard the newborn as a source of interest. Our memories, even subconscious ones, dim with age as they become woven into more and more complex behavior patterns. Thus, to wait until a child is an adult before explaining fetal life to him is to strain his comprehension unnecessarily. He will accept the whole fetal and newborn situation with much greater understanding when his own subconscious experience of it is fresher. The small child retains his familiarity with beat and rhythm from fetal experience of them. His early speech has a metrical quality. Like the new baby, he has, before birth, listened to the pulse beat more than to any other sound. He lapped, swallowed, perhaps even moved about in the womb, rhythmically. If he hiccoughed, it had a rhythm. Following birth, there is rhythm to his cry, the way he suckles, swallows, and breathes. On a wider pattern there is rhythm to his sleep and his hunger. Is it little wonder that one so accustomed to beat and rhythm can obtain emotional satisfaction from the soothing sound of a lullaby or from the lulling sensation of gentle rocking? Through these rhythmic responses he establishes a wider range of communication with his mother.

Properly the mother should introduce her child to the fact that there is a new baby on the way when the fetus is big enough to be readily felt. When the baby does arrive and needs frequent attention, the wise mother will make room on her rocking chair for the ex-baby too, rather than trying to distract this older child from the rocking and lullaby he once loved so well. The chances are that his constant thirst for knowledge will provide such a distraction that he has no cause to fear that he has lost his mother's protection.

Freud held that fetal and newborn life were psychologically a continuum, with a caesura occurring at birth. Certainly both phases leave their imprint indelibly, and the greater our understanding of early joys and fears, the more likely will we all be able to tune in on the same wavelength.

Fetology, the youngest branch of medicine and one that deals with the youngest patients, holds many secret parcels. Some developments, of course, are predictable. There will be an increasingly better assessment of the effects of birth on the course of the baby's subsequent life. And there will be a greater awareness that it is the baby who conducts the orchestra in pregnancy, and that we should be able to predict his condition more accurately by studying the ways in which he is affecting his host's body.

The problem of maternal survival is no longer a major concern in modern obstetrics. Fetal survival, too, has reached a sufficiently high percentage that it has ceased to be the principal aim. Today's problems concern a more thorough understanding of the unborn baby, so that we can provide help for the baby born too soon, and the baby born with some serious damage. All that we know thus far still needs to be applied.

To diagnose babies before birth; be able to treat them at that time; and thus provide them the best promise of future health, we must bend every effort toward a better understanding of their ageless, unchanging fetal environment. It seems ironic that we can know more about the minute-to-minute physiological condition of our monitored astronauts, whirling around in space thousands of miles away from us, than we as yet know about the unborn baby who lies but an inch or two away from our eyes.

Childbirth is indeed still both a miracle and a mystery. The challenge facing medicine today is to make it less of a mystery, and, as the shrouds surrounding pregnancy and birth are pushed back by science, to let the miracle be even more clearly seen.

To do this, it is of the greatest importance that intra-uterine life be regarded as a continuum with extra-uterine life, and infancy with childhood. The phases are not distinct for the individual, but merge. The baby demands comfort before birth and for many weeks following birth. He is the chairman, his mother a hard-working committee member.

Her reward is, for a little while, to be everything to someone: provider, decision maker, philosopher, tutor, and friend.

APPENDIX OF PRACTICALITIES

DIET

Protein foods are body builders and are a must in pregnancy. Meat, fish, eggs, cheese, nuts, and some milk (½ to 1 pint per day) are the best sources of protein. It is advisable to broil rather than fry meats, to remove excess fat, and to exclude cream. Fresh fruits and vegetables are a daily requirement. Since the fluid requirement is doubled in pregnancy, this means more tea, coffee, water, soft drinks, and more fruit.

Each day's menu should include:
1. Milk—1 glass or more.
2. One or more servings of lean meat, poultry, fish, and eggs.
3. One or more servings of green or yellow leafy vegetables.
4. Fresh fruit, one or more servings.
5. Other vegetables, fruits, including potatoes, dried fruits, etc., one serving.
6. Cereals and breads. One or more servings, depending on weight.

Foods to avoid:
Oils, fats, cream, fried foods, excess sweets and pastries. This is true even for women who are not weight-watchers, since the incidence of some forms of toxemia is increased in populations where fats and oils are used heavily in cooking.

HAVE YOUR BABY—AND YOUR FIGURE

Ante Natal

Posture is extremely important throughout pregnancy since good posture will prevent undue stretching of abdominal muscles and back strain. A woman should keep her back straight and make herself as tall as possible at all times, whether sitting, standing, or walking. She also should choose shoes for comfort and support; spending long periods in high heels will throw her off balance.

Start the following exercise and continue them from the first three months of pregnancy. Each exercise should be held for the count of five and done five times every day. These exercises are designed to strengthen muscles that get stretched during pregnancy (abdominal muscles) or during birth of baby (pelvic floor muscles, especially around the vagina).

Lying on Back:

(*a*) *Pelvic tilting. Lying on back, one leg crossed over the other. Pull in tummy, tuck seat under so that hollow of back flattens against the floor, squeeze tops of thighs together, and pull up pelvic floor muscles as if controlling bladder.*

(*b*) Feet apart, still lying. Stretch right arm up and over toward left big toe so that the head and shoulders lift from floor. Lower slowly and repeat with other arm.

Kneeling:

(*a*) Humping and hollowing. Pull tummy and tuck head and seat down, then slowly hollow back and bring head and seat up.

(*b*) Wiggle waggle. Turn head toward seat, to the left, and then to the right.

Standing:

Pelvic tilting. As in first exercise, but now in standing position with one leg crossed in front of the other.

Squatting:

Keep back straight and knees apart. Practice this only once a week to relax inner thigh muscles. Use this position when lifting, i.e., bend knees rather than back.

LABOR AND BIRTH

Start these exercises in the last three months of pregnancy, with a tutor if possible.

Breathing:

A. *Rhythmic deep breathing:* this has a calming effect and relaxes the muscles throughout the body. Deep breathing may be approached in two ways:

Abdominal breathing:

Lie on back with pillow under head and knees bent up; place both hands on tummy (above umbilicus). Breathe in through nose and lift abdominal wall up. Breathe out through relaxed lips and unclenched teeth and your abdominal wall will sink down.

Costal breathing:

Lie on back with pillow under head and knees bent up; place hands at sides of ribs. Breathe in through nose and feel your ribs move sideways against your hands. Breathe out through relaxed lips and unclenched teeth and feel your ribs move away from your hands.

The speed of both abdominal and costal breathing is four to six breaths per thirty seconds. This breathing is used for the first stage of labor when the cervix (or sphincter muscle) is stretching (or dilating).

B. *Controlled "panting" breathing:* Lie as before in (A), but you may prefer to prop up your head and shoulders with two pillows. Let your lips just part, your teeth unclench, and your tongue lie loosely on floor of mouth; head should be "heavy."

The speed of this breathing is thirty- to thirty-five breaths per thirty seconds. Beware of breathing too deeply. This breathing is used for the middle or peak of the first stage, and for the birth of baby's head in the second stage; it should be practiced each day during pregnancy.

Relaxation:

Lie on side with underneath arm tucked right under behind you. First tense all muscles and then relax to feel the difference. Later progress to relaxing completely without tensing up first. You may use a pillow under forward knee also if more comfortable.

In the first stage of labor, lie in the relaxation position in your hospital bed and use abdominal or costal breathing during each contraction.

Panting breathing is used at the end of the first stage and while the baby's head is being born.

How to bear down:

(i.e., push baby out to be born) When you practice this your baby is high under your chest, but when the real time comes, the baby is low in your abdomen, so it is much easier to bear down then.

Part 1 for Bearing Down

Be propped up with two or three pillows:

Breathe **in** through **nose** and out through **mouth**
Breathe **in** through **mouth** and hold that breath for ten counts
Breathe **out** through **mouth** gently
Breathe **in** through **mouth** and hold that breath for ten counts
Breathe **out** through **mouth** gently
Breathe **in** through **mouth** and hold that breath for ten counts
Breathe **out** through **mouth** gently

and rest.

The time when you hold your breath is the time when you push on the day of birth: do not push when practicing—only hold breath to ten counts as explained above.

Part 2 for Bearing Down

Be propped up with pillows:

Pull knees up and out toward armpits, put hands under thighs, let knees "flop" out and pelvic floor relax ("come down"). Lift chin onto chest.

Combine Part 1 with Part 2 for full rehearsal of bearing down.

POST NATAL

Start these exercises a day or two after the birth of the baby if you feel up to it. Hold each exercise for the count of five and do each one five times daily for three months.

Your Posture:

Check this very carefully, as it has to be adjusted to your new shape. Stand tall with your tummy held in. Spend half an hour every day lying on your tummy. If necessary, put a pillow under your hips. When at home it may be more convenient to spend a short time lying on your tummy before going to sleep. This will encourage the uterus to return to its normal position while it is contracting to its original size.

Exercises:

Start as soon as you feel like it, after the birth. Lie on your back, with knees bent. Pull your tummy and let go.

Second day:

(1) *Pelvic tilting.*
Lying on back, one leg
crossed over the other.
Pull in tummy, tuck seat
under so that hollow of
back flattens against floor,
squeeze tops of thighs
together and pull up
pelvic floor muscles as if
controlling bladder.

Third day:

(1) *as for second day.*
(2) *Lie on back.*
Stretch right arm up and
over toward left toe,
so that head and
shoulders lift from floor.
Lower slowly and
repeat with other arm.

Fourth day.

(1) and (2) as for third day
(3) *Lie on back, with knees straight. Lift alternate legs slowly off bed and lower them slowly.*

Fifth day onward:

(1) and (2) as for third day. (4) *Lie on back, with knees bent, feet on floor. Raise head and hands to knees, lower slowly.*

Vaginal Lavage and Control:

After the local discharge has ceased, lie in a bath half-filled with clean water. Draw in tummy wall and the pelvic floor as in the pelvic tilting exercise. If all is in order, water should be drawn into the vagina. Expel it with bearing-down pressure. This is an excellent exercise for prevention of forms of prolapse.

LAYETTE

Clothing needs vary so much from season to season and place to place that a list can indicate no more than basic requirements.

6 undershirts. Cotton, open at side or front. Six-months size.

4 Gowns, made of a warm material such as flannel, for use both day and night during the first three or four months. Six-months size.

2 baby blankets, the one to alternate while the other is being washed.

4 Receiving blankets. Cotton.

2 Washcloths. Terry, soft.

2 Towels. Terry, soft.

2 Crib sheets.

Bath equipment. Soap dish, mild soap, mineral oil, absorbent cotton, safety pins, talcum powder. Desitin or similar ointment for rash.

Baby can be bathed in washstand or kitchen sink.

2 sweaters. 1 heavy wool and one light wool.

3 dozen diapers. (Keep a dozen on hand even if you have a diaper service.)

3 or 4 pairs leggings-suits of cotton knit or stretch suits.

3 flannel squares, to go over the diapers when the baby is being put down to sleep. (Plastic pants are liable to produce a rash.)

2 8-ounce bottles and 4 firm nipples.

Mittens and a bonnet may be needed for winter babies.

Crib and firm mattress.

1 Mattress cover, waterproof.

Carriage:

A large one has the advantage of providing an alternative, and often convenient, sleeping place for the baby for many months. When left to sleep in the open, the baby should be protected from flies, etc., by a piece of netting draped over the open portion.

Clothes for mother to have packed, ready for hospital:

2 nightgowns
1 bed jacket
1 dressing gown, washable and not too long
1 pair slippers
Hairbrush and comb, toothbrush, toothpaste, washcloth, soap, and
         dusting powder
1 sanitary belt
2 nursing brassieres

Clothing for baby to bring to hospital:

3 diapers with diaper pins
1 nightgown
1 quilted pad or plastic pants
1 shirt
1 cotton receiving blanket
1 wool blanket
1 sweater and cap

HOW TO BREAST-FEED THE NEW BABY

0–2 days: breast for one minute, three to four times in twenty-four hours; then offer sugar and water.

2 days–2 or 3 weeks: breast and/or bottle three to five minutes each side or until baby is satisfied, five to seven times in twenty-four hours.

Third week–third month (approximately): baby will gradually develop his own routine. If he wants more than five feeds now, then he is probably getting an insufficient amount. Substitute one or more breast feeds for a bottle feed made as follows:

4 ounces homogenized milk
2 ounces boiling water
2 teaspoons sugar

Sterilization: Bottles and nipples are kept germ-free by *either* heat sterilization (boiling) *or* chemical sterilization (Milton method).

NOTE:
At first baby will not necessarily awaken for food at the *same time* each day but the *same number* of times in the day.

At two months of age most babies are ready for regularized feeding.

Dainty feeders take small meals and seem satisfied, but they tend to awaken more frequently than five or six times in the day. Encourage such babies to have a little rest after a feed and then suckle again.

Hungry babies may sometimes overflow after feeding and are prone to hiccups.

Always prepare nipples and wait one minute before letting baby suckle to allow time for the milk to be let down. Don't forget to cleanse your breasts after feeding also.

Weight gain is variable. There is usually some loss in the first few days and then a gain of from one-half to one and one-half ounces daily.

HOW TO BOTTLE-FEED THE NEW BABY

0–2 days: sugar and water three to four times in twenty-four hours. Formula may be offered after the first day if baby seems hungry.

2 days–3 weeks: bottle five to seven times in twenty-four hours.

After the third week, the baby will gradually develop his own routine. He should not require more than five feedings daily (twenty-four hours).

Formula can be made either of homogenized milk or powdered baby milk. Powdered milk is safest when traveling.

Always wash hands after changing the baby and before preparing his milk mixture or handling his feeding utensils. All utensils must be sterilized before use.

Formula Made with Fresh Milk

Multiples of this ratio:	2 ounces homogenized milk to
	1 ounce water and
	1 teaspoon sugar
Thus, the supply for one day would be:	20 ounces milk
	10 ounces water
	10 teaspoons sugar

Method:

1. Measure the sugar and dissolve it in the boiling water.
2. Stir milk, measure amount needed and add it to the sugar-water solution.
3. Bring the mixture just to the boiling point, in a clean saucepan kept just for this purpose.
4. Simmer for five minutes. Cool. Pour equally into sterilized bottles. Use six bottles per day until the baby is three weeks old, then five until the baby sleeps all night, when four are sufficient.

Formula Made with Powdered Milk

Since powdered baby milk contains sugar, usually no additional sugar is necessary. Commercial brands generally contain their own measure, and directions for amount of water (usually 1 tablespoon of milk powder to 2 ounces of water).

Method:

1. Measure required amount of powdered milk. Mix to a smooth paste with a small amount of boiled water. When quite smooth, add sufficient boiling water to make total quantity.

2. Pour into sterilized container and cool rapidly.
3. Keep covered in refrigerator. Pour desired amount into bottle and warm it in pan of hot water. Test temperature by shaking a few drops on your wrist. Milk should be body temperature.

NOTE: Always use a level measure of powdered milk, not heaped. Discard whatever the baby leaves and rinse the bottle. Do not smoke while feeding the baby.

HOW TO BATHE THE BABY

Preparation:
1. Keep all bath items together.
2. A terry cloth apron will protect your clothes.
3. The room should be warm and not drafty.
4. Clean clothes should be put out for the baby.
5. The water should be tested with your elbow—it should feel pleasantly warm.

Bath:
1. Wash baby's face with a clean soft cloth. Do not use soap.
2. Soap baby's head. Then, holding him in a dry towel, place the head gently over the side of the bath and sponge the soap off the head.
3. Dry the head.
4. Now soap baby's body, particularly in the creases.
5. Place baby right in the water but be careful to support the back and head on your arm.
6. When possible allow baby time to have fun in the bath.
7. Pat the baby dry with a soft towel, again being careful to dry in creases and behind neck and ears.

It is usual to bathe the baby in the morning while he is very young, but later an evening bath will help him sleep at night.

Index

About the Author

D R . H . M . I . L I L E Y was born and educated in New Zealand and is the wife of Dr. A. William Liley, the obstetrician whose technique for transfusing the unborn baby has saved the lives of countless infants. Dr. Liley practices medicine in New Zealand, is the mother of five children and the Director of the Ante-Natal Clinic at the National Women's Hospital in Auckland.

Dr. Liley's work in educating expectant mothers in the facts of the fetal and newborn life is the result of her conviction of "the essential dignity of this smallest parcel of humanity." She writes: "To become a parent is the greatest of privileges . . . immortalizing something of oneself in a child is the reward of all who influence the very young. Those within a family contribute an imprint which will never be erased. It is only through knowledge that we can face parenthood responsibly."

B E T H D A Y is an accomplished writer of articles and books. She is the author of fifteen published works and has contributed to such magazines as *McCall's, Reader's Digest, Parents' Magazine, Ladies Home Journal* and *Woman's Day.*